God's
Divine Instructions To Husbands and Men

God's
Divine Instructions To Husbands and Men

AELTON SIMMONS

Copyright © 2021 by Aelton Simmons.

All rights reserved. No part of this publication may be reproduced, distributed, or transmitted in any form or by any means, including photocopying, recording, or other electronic or mechanical methods, without the prior written permission of the author, except in the case of brief quotations embodied in critical reviews and certain other noncommercial uses permitted by copyright law.

All scripture quotations, unless otherwise specified, are from the King James Version of the Holy Bible.

Printed in the United States of America

ISBN 978-1-64133-666-6 (paperback)

LCCN: 2021923552

Inspirational

MainSpring Books
5901 W. Century Blvd
Suite 750
Los Angeles, CA, US, 90045
www.mainspringbooks.com

FOR MORE INFORMATION, PLEASE CONTACT:

A. C. Simmons
962 Kingswood Estate
Pine Bluff, AR 71613
870-329-0956

CONTENTS

Chapter 1	Ten Things a Husband Must Do to Help Make His Marriage a Success	5
Chapter 2	Being a Faithful Husband Who Fulfills His Duties and Yields to His Wife's Needs and Desires 1st Corinthians 7:2-4	19
Chapter 3	The Husband Is To Be His Wife's Lover and the Spiritual Head of His Family	31
Chapter 4	Holding On to and Sanctifying Your Wife	47
Chapter 5	Husbands Living Right for Their Children and Seeking to Please Their Wives	59
Chapter 6	Leading and Loving Your Wife like Christ Does the Church	69
Chapter 7	Giving Yourself Totally to Your Wife	83
Chapter 8	Loving Your Wife as Yourself and Leaving Your Parents	93
Chapter 9	Uniting as One Flesh with Your Wife	103
Chapter 10	Guarding Against Bitterness	117
Chapter 11	Dwelling with Your Wife according to Knowledge	133
Chapter 12	Giving Honor to Your Wife	147
Chapter 13	Heirs Together of the Grace of Life	155
Chapter 14	Receiving the Right Wife	169
Chapter 15	Things That a Husband Should Never Do (Part 1)	181

Chapter 16 Things That a Husband Should Never Do (Part 2) 189

Chapter 17 A Word to Those Who Have Been
            Divorced and Remarried 197

Chapter 18 What Is a Man, and What Is a Man Supposed to Do? 211

Chapter 19 What Is a Man, and What Is a Man Supposed to Do?
            (Part 2) 225

Chapter 20 Spiritual Checklists for Husbands and Men 237

DEDICATION

This book is dedicated to my father, Fred Simmons Jr. and to my mother, Josephine Simmons, who have revealed to me the wisdom and knowledge needed to successfully write this book. They have live out in their marriage the marital principles discussed in this book, and have shown me that it is possible to have a lasting and successful marriage. It is also dedicated to my wife Brenda who have worked with me through love, prayer, patience, and the written Word of God to transform me into the man and husband I am today. It is also dedicated to my children and grandchildren whom I love, cherish, and adore with all my heart.

This book is dedicated to my heavenly Father, who loves me with an everlasting, un-merited, maximized love. It is dedicated to my Lord and Savior Jesus Christ who died for me to save my soul. It is dedicated to the Holy Spirit who anointed me with wisdom, knowledge, and ability to write this book.

Lastly, this book is dedicated to husbands and men who desire to be all God desires them to be. I pray God will use this book in your spiritual, mental, and physical maturity. May the blessings of God richly bless you and develop you into that which is well pleasing in His sight.

(Hebrews. 13:20-21) [20]*Now the God of peace, that brought again from the dead our Lord Jesus, that great shepherd of the sheep, through the blood of the everlasting covenant,* [21]*Make you perfect in every good work to do his will, working in you that which is wellpleasing in his sight, through Jesus Christ; to whom be glory for ever and ever. Amen.*

Jesus is LORD

INTRODUCTION

To have a successful marriage, every husband must know what a successful marriage is, and he must be armed with the proper information on how to cause his marriage to be a success. A successful marriage is one that lasts a lifetime, and possesses all that the Holy Bible says a marriage is to possess. It is a marriage filled with love, communication, romance, spiritual growth, victory over difficulties, and all of the other things that are part of a wonderful marriage. Sexual fulfillment, laughter, togetherness, and peace are also a part of such a marriage. Everything a man would want for his marriage (that is in agreement with the Word of God) is a part of what a successful marriage is.

A successful marriage is a marriage every husband has the potential of having if he does things according to the Word of God. Salvation, obedience to God, the power of the Holy Ghost, and your faith in God are all of the necessary ingredients needed to produce a successful and fulfilling marriage. As a husband, you must learn how to take these things and use them to seek to create the kind of marriage that you and God will both be well pleased with.

Far too often, men try to build their marriages on what they think are the right things to do; still, the marriage ends up in un-fulfillment, discontentment, and, sometimes, divorce. In spite of the energy and effort they invest into the marriage, it still turns into a bad marriage because they did things their way and not God's way. However, there are some things that you can do to avoid having a bad marriage. If your marriage is already considered bad, there are things you can do to turn it into a wonderful, blessed, and successful marriage. There is nothing impossible for God; if you are God's child who will trust Him and obey His Word, it will not be impossible to turn a bad marriage into a blessed marriage.

God's Divine Instructions to Husbands and Men is a book geared toward informing men on what their role in marriage is, and how to fulfill that role.

God's Divine Instructions To Husbands and Men

It will show you where you may have been in error concerning your marriage and also areas in which you may need to improve. While the information in this book is based on the Word of God, it will not benefit you until you learn these things and then implement them into your life and marriage. If you want a fulfilling and successful marriage, it is time to abandon your ideas and thoughts about a husband's role in marriage, and adopt God's Divine instructions from His Word as it deals with the role of a husband in marriage.

Father; please use this book for the spiritual growth and edification of husbands and men. Please open their hearts of understanding, their ears of hearing, and their minds of remembrance, so they can daily apply into their lives the truths found written in the pages of this book. In Jesus' name I pray; amen.

Jesus my LORD; thank You for empowering husbands and men to walk in victory in their marriages, homes, and lives. Thank You for using Your written Word, the Holy Spirit, and this book, to advance husbands and men to higher and higher levels of wisdom, power, authority, and dominion in Your name. May You and the Father be glorified through this book by the power of the Holy Spirit.

CHAPTER 1

Ten Things a Husband Must Do to Help Make His Marriage a Success

1. Always put God first in your life and marriage.

2. Always do your part even if your wife is not doing her part.

3. You must be committed to trying to make the marriage the best it can be even when it seems that the feelings of love are gone.

4. It is more your responsibility to strive to make the marriage all that it can be than it is the responsibility of your wife.

5. Learn to communicate with your wife in a fruitful and productive way.

6. Seek to keep romance, excitement, and togetherness in your marriage.

7. Always be ready for spiritual warfare because the devil will sooner or later attack your marriage to try to destroy it.

8. Try to learn about and to understand the physical and mental changes that your wife goes through during PMS and menopause.

God's Divine Instructions To Husbands and Men

9. Keeping a fulfilling sexual relationship between you and your wife is going to be a challenge (especially as you get older) that you must constantly work at if it is going to stay fresh, exciting, and fulfilling.

10. Beware of the things that most commonly destroy a marriage.

Aelton Simmons

Ten Things a Husband Must Do to Help Make His Marriage a Success

In every successful marriage, there are certain key elements that exist that will aid in making that marriage a success. Without these key elements, hardships and problems can arise, which can be contributing factors to the destruction of that marriage. Every marriage needs a solid foundation to build on. The key elements to a successful marriage, which we will discuss in this section of our book, will help to build the solid foundation that your marriage will need to stand on. Check your life and marriage to see if these things exist there. If they do not, start putting them into your life and marriage now. The key elements we will discuss in this section of our book are not all of the ingredients needed to build a successful marriage on, but they are enough to start with. Throughout this book, we will be discussing many other things that you as a husband will need to do. Everything needs a starting point; these key elements should be your starting point to a successful marriage.

1. Always put God first in your life and marriage.

It is not you who will make your marriage a success; it is God working in you, in your spouse, and in your marriage that will make it a success. In order for God to work in your marriage, someone in the marriage must first be a Christian. If you are not a Christian, your marriage will never reach the fullness of what it could be. If you are the one desiring for your marriage to be the best it can be, you must first become a Christian, and then you must seek to obey what God says a husband is to do.

To become a Christian, there are three major things you must do:

You must believe that Jesus Christ is the only begotten son of God who died on the cross for the sins of the world, and three days later, God raised him from the dead.

You must be willing to repent of (turn away from) your sins and of satan, and turn to Jesus Christ and the righteousness He brings.

Confess with your mouth that you want Jesus Christ to forgive you of your sins, to come and live in your heart by faith, and to become the Lord and Savior of your life.

To become saved, you must believe, be willing to repent of sin and satan, and then confess that you want Jesus Christ as your personal Lord and Savior. If you have never asked Jesus to save you, you are not saved; you will end up in hell, and you will not have God working in you to help make your marriage a success. Once you become saved and begin learning (and doing) what God says to do, God will begin to work to help make your marriage the best it can be. Always put God first in everything, and you will always have God working to help make your marriage and your life a success. Never forget that success in marriage and in life always begins with God. Have you put God first place in your life and marriage yet?

2. Always do your part even if your wife is not doing her part.

God never tells you to get your wife to do her part in marriage before you begin doing your part. God commands certain things for you to do, and you are responsible for doing those things regardless of what your wife is doing. Your actions are not to be reactions to your wife's actions; your actions are to be reactions of obedience to what God tells you to do. Do what God says to do, and leave your wife in the hands of God. If God does not change her into what she should be, you will not be able to change her into what she should be.

The spouse that is doing his or her part, as God has commanded, is usually the one who is keeping the marriage together. If your wife is not doing her part in the marriage and you refuse to do your part, God will have no one to work through; difficulties will come in, and the marriage may end up in divorce. To do your part as a husband, you must learn what your part is. To learn what your part in marriage is, read the Holy Bible, talk to your pastor, read books such as this one, listen to sermons, and talk to older godly couples that have a successful marriage. Talk to them so you can learn the secret of their success. Do all you can to learn what God says your part in marriage is, and then fulfill your part.

Fulfilling your part when your wife is not fulfilling her part is not always an easy thing to do. It takes prayer, patience, and endurance. It also takes faith in God. Along with prayer, patience, endurance, and faith, you will need (1) self-discipline, (2) an unending determination and dedication, and (3) much sacrifice.

There will be times when you will not feel like doing what you are supposed to do as a husband, but if you want to fulfill the Word of God and make your marriage the best it can be; always do your part even when you don't feel like it, and even when your wife is not doing her part.

3. You must be committed to trying to make the marriage the best it can be even when it seems that the feelings of love are gone.

There must always be more commitment in marriage than feelings of love. Feelings of love are emotions that can change with circumstances and situations. Feelings of love can increase, decrease, and, at times, can even vanish completely. When the feelings are small and at times are gone, you as a husband must be committed to doing your part. You need to be the one trying to keep the marriage together, and you must be the one seeking to do what is needed to rebuild the feelings of love that you had for your wife and that she had for you.

Commitment is a none ending dedication and determination to accomplishing something as long as it is in your power to accomplish it. As long as you and her are together, you must have a commitment to always work to make the marriage the best it can be. Never let anything or anyone cause you to lose your commitment to your wife, to your marriage, and to your God.

4. It is more your responsibility to strive to make the marriage all that it can be than it is the responsibility of your wife.

As the husband, you are the head of the marriage; and thus, the greater responsibility for trying to make the marriage a success rests on you. When things are wrong in the marriage, God may deal with you before He begins to deal with your wife. God expects more out of you than He does out of her. You bear the responsibility of doing what it takes to establish and to keep in your marriage, love, romance, communication, unity, spiritual growth, and all of the other things that should be in a marriage. If these things are gone from your marriage, it is never to be your fault, and you must continue trying to restore these things. To be a husband carries great responsibilities that your wife will never know of, nor will she ever be required to fulfill, nor could she fulfill.

Although you carry the greater responsibility, that does not relieve your wife of doing her part in the marriage. God holds her responsible for performing her duties, and performing them with her whole heart. When she fails to fulfill her role, she will lose her joy, contentment, and many of her blessings. God will also begin to chasten her in ways that will cause her to yield the peaceable fruits of righteousness.

[11].*Now no chastening for the present seemeth to be joyous, but grievous: nevertheless afterward it yieldeth the peaceable fruit of righteousness unto them which are exercised thereby. (Hebrews. 12:11)*

5. Learn to communicate with your wife in fruitful and productive ways.

Communication in marriage is a key element that can often make the difference between loving discussions and heated arguments. The way a thing is said and the time it is said is of great importance in marriage. Many marriages are in trouble today because of a lack of proper communication skills. Communication involves talking and listening. Each spouse needs to learn how to talk in an acceptable way and how to listen in the right manner. Do not engage in any type of meaningful conversation when angry because speaking out of anger may cause you to say things you really do not mean, things you really shouldn't have said, and things that take a long time for you and your wife to overcome. Learn to always let your speech be seasoned with grace and love. Look for the right way, look for the right time, and look for the right place for whatever conversation you wish to engage in.

Realize that listening is also a key part of conversation. Every wife wants to know that when she is talking, her husband is listening with un-distracted ears. Don't always try to give her answers and advice because sometimes, she is not seeking for answers and advice. There are times when she just wants someone to be there to listen to what she has to say. Work at setting aside special moments so you and she can talk. Go to places and do things together that will allow both of you to talk and unburden your souls to one another.

Learn to communicate with your wife in nonverbal ways. Hugging, kissing, holding each other, giving gifts for no special reason, and doing other silent gestures of love are acts of nonverbal communication that are constantly needed in a marriage. Doing things she asks you to do and doing things she does not ask but you know she wants done are some of the best and most meaningful kinds of communications you can do without speaking a word. Oftentimes, what you do, speaks louder than what you say.

6. Seek to keep romance, excitement, and togetherness in your marriage.

Some of the major reasons many husbands have extramarital affairs are because they are seeking for (1) romance and sexual fulfillment, (2) someone who will do fun and exciting things with them, (3) someone who will make them feel special and important, and (4) someone with whom they can talk. One of the major reasons they give for their affairs is that they do not get these things at home, so they must seek them elsewhere.

Husbands, it is never for you to seek these things elsewhere. It is for you to work to establish these things in your home with your wife. Also, you are to do what it takes to keep these things in your home. Having romance, excitement, and togetherness in your marriage is not something that will happen automatically; these are things that you as a husband must strive for and work toward. It begins with making a commitment to yourself that you will constantly do what it takes to keep them in your marriage. Once your mind is made up to do so, it will require much planning, creativeness, hard work, and prayer.

What are you doing to keep romance, excitement, and togetherness in your marriage? Are you still dating your wife and saying sweet and wonderful things to her and about her? Do you take her out to dinner and give her gifts when she least expects it? When you get to the point in your marriage where you stop doing these things, you will get to the point where romance, excitement, and togetherness will begin to fade.

Go back to dating and romancing your wife. Try to develop things that you and she can do together. Sit down and think of things to do, get suggestions from others, read books, and also ask your wife what things she would like to do. Remember to always pray to God, asking Him to help you do what is needed to keep romance, excitement, and togetherness in your marriage.

Once when I was looking for a job and could not find one, my father told me that when you cannot find a job, go and make a job for yourself. If you cannot find romance, excitement, and togetherness in your marriage, then go and make romance, excitement, and togetherness in your marriage because these are things that can be done.

7. Always be ready for spiritual warfare because the devil will sooner or later attack your marriage to try to destroy it.

The devil hates godly marriages and will, at times, attack your marriage to try to destroy it, thus you must always be ready for spiritual battles. In order to destroy your marriage, the devil will try to use you, your wife, other people, and circumstances. If he cannot get you to act wrong, he will try to get your wife to do things that will cause problems in the marriage. He will also try to use others to do things that will cause you and your wife to be at odds with each other. If using people fail, he will use circumstances such as financial problems, misunderstandings, and divided interests and desires. He will do all he can, with what he can, to try to destroy your marriage.

When things happen in your marriage that has the potential of destroying your marriage, those things that are happening are the workings of the devil. When you notice the devil at work, it is not time to fight against your wife; it is time to fight against the devil. Always love your wife, and always fight the devil. Always treat your wife with love and tenderness, and always treat the devil as a hated enemy to be defeated. When problems arise, pray about them with your wife first, then sit down and, in love, discuss it together. Always remember she is never your enemy, and you are never to treat her as though she is.

Learn to fight victoriously against the devil and his demons. Learn how to put on the whole armor of God (Ephesians.6:10-18) and how to use the weapons of your warfare (2nd Corinthians. 10:3-6). Always quote what the Word of God says about your marriage, and cover your marriage with the blood of Jesus Christ. You cover your marriage with the blood of Jesus by (1) dedicating your marriage to God and (2) obeying what God says in His written Word. When you always do the things God says in His Word that a husband is to do, the devil will not be able to destroy your marriage. Jesus promised that if you build your house (and marriage) upon hearing and obeying the Word of God, when the storms of the devil come and blow against your house (and marriage), it will stand the storm without falling and being destroyed (Matthew. 7:24-27).

8. Try to learn about and to understand the physical and mental changes that your wife goes through during PMS and menopause.

PMS (premenstrual syndrome) and menopause are physical changes that occur within a woman's body that affects her mental attitude. These are powerful changes that usually cause a woman to become irritable and place her in a mood of not wanting to be bothered by anyone. She goes through different emotional changes that her husband usually does not understand; thus, he thinks she is upset with him and is rejecting him. The truth of the matter is that she is dealing with these powerful changes in the best way she knows how.

During these changes, her sex drive decreases, and she is not in the mood for romance or anything else. You, the children, everything, and everyone get on her nerves; and she just wants to be left alone. Husbands, when your wife goes through these changes, you must exercise patience; and you must realize she is not rejecting you, but she is experiencing some hard things physically that she has to deal with. If you give her space and time, she will soon get over those changes and will be back to treating you the way she usually does. Don't react in anger; react in love, and when these changes have passed, she may show her appreciation for your patience during her times of physical and emotional changes.

9. Keeping a fulfilling sexual relationship between you and your wife is going to be a challenge (especially as you get older) that you must constantly work at if it is going to stay fresh, exciting, and fulfilling.

One of the biggest challenges that you as a husband will face is the challenge of trying to keep your wife satisfied sexually. It is so easy for us as men to receive sexual gratification that we can fall into the trap of thinking that it should be just as easy for our wives to be gratified. Many wives' sexual natures are much lower than that of men's, and thus, it takes much more for her to be sexually satisfied.

Husbands, never fail to do the things needed to keep your sexual relationship with your wife exciting and fulfilling. Learn what you must do, don't fall into a routine, and don't take for granted that she is satisfied. Remember, sexual fulfillment for a woman starts with her emotions. Also, remember that foreplay doesn't begin in the bedroom at the end of the day; it begins at the beginning of the day and lasts all day long. Your wife must be mentally and emotionally ready before she can become physically ready.

A man is sexually aroused by sight and touch, even if his emotions have been disturbed in a negative way. If a wife's emotions have been disturbed in a negative way, it is almost impossible for her to receive sexual satisfaction. Deal with her emotionally before trying to deal with her physically. Set the mood for love by constantly giving her compliments, by constantly helping around the house, and by constantly showing her gestures of your love for her.

As you (and she) grow older (especially after the age of forty), it will become increasingly harder to please her sexually. Her sex drive decreases dramatically, and sex is no longer an important thing to her. She will not want sexual involvement as much, and it will take much more to please her. When these times come, realize that it was her sex drive that decreased and not her love for you. Don't go seeking sexual satisfaction elsewhere; get used to having sex less, work harder on pleasing her, and focus more on loving her than making love to her. Also, remember that while it may be harder to please her sexually, it will not be impossible; it will just take greater commitment and more effort than before.

10. Beware of things that most commonly destroy a marriage.

Beware of financial strains.

One of the major reasons many marriages end is because of the financial strains that may occur in a marriage, and the couple's inability to properly deal with them. When financial problems occur, regardless of whose fault it is, the couple must work together to overcome them and not begin fighting against each other. Overcome the financial strains, and do not let the financial strains overcome the marriage. Work on creating a budget, while seeking ways to increase income and reduce expenses.

Beware of arguments and how you handle them.

There will be times when you and your wife will disagree. During these times of disagreement, tempers will flare, and anger will arise. Try to calm down before dealing with whatever is causing the problem. Never call each other bad names, and do not try to cast all of the blame on the other person. Both may be at fault, and usually, no one is 100% right. Learn to compromise for love sake, and for peace sake, and realize that you still love each other even though you do not agree on everything.

Beware of addictions.

Being addicted to drugs, alcohol, and other chemicals puts a big strain on a marriage and has the potential to destroy a marriage. If you are not yet addicted to these things, do not start using them. You never have to stop doing something that you never started doing. If you are already addicted to these things, get help so you can break the addiction. Also being addicted to work and other things can destroy a marriage as well. When you begin to do more for other people and other things than you do for your wife, you may be addicted to those things, and you are on the way to destroying your marriage. Never put anything before your wife but God because anything else you may put before her may be the thing the devil uses to try to destroy your marriage.

Beware of being unfaithful.

Never get involved in an outside sexual relationship because it will be discovered and it may destroy your marriage. Do what it takes to stay away from temptations. Seek to love your wife and your God so much that you can overcome any temptation that may come your way. Faithfulness in marriage must be one of the major priorities for husbands and wives.

Beware of the negative outside influence of other people.

Do not let someone outside of your home try to tell you how to act within your home. Your guide for marriage is found in the Word of God. Do not discuss the problems that you are having in the marriage with people outside the marriage unless that person is your professional counselor. Many marriages would be much better if it were not for the outside influences of other people. The three main groups of outsiders to be aware of are the following: (1) parents (especially mothers because many sons do not let go of their mothers' apron strings, and many mothers do not let go of their sons); (2) close friends, partners, and buddies; and (3) past and present lovers.

Father; to know these things but not do them will profit no one. Please prompt husbands and men to be diligent in performing the things You are teaching them through this book. Please work powerfully, mightily, and diligently to transform husbands and men into the kind of husbands and men you desire them to be. May they constantly increase in Jesus Christ to Your glory by the power of the Holy Spirit. In Jesus' name I pray; amen.

[17]*If ye know these things, happy are ye if ye do them. (John.13:17).*

Jesus my LORD: husbands and men can no longer afford to allow the enemy of our souls to destroy our marriages, children, churches, businesses, societies, and lives. Because of the victory You secured for us on the Cross of Calvary, we will no longer allow the devil to have his way. Thank you for using this book as part of what You are doing to empower husbands and men to bind, rebuke, and cast out the enemy. Thank You for using this book as part of what you are doing to empower men to walk in, live in, and flow in greater levels of authority, power, and dominion.

¹*Then he called his twelve disciples together, and gave them power and authority over all devils, and to cure diseases. (Luke.9:1)*

¹⁴*And he ordained twelve, that they should be with him, and that he might send them forth to preach,* ¹⁵*And to have power to heal sicknesses, and to cast out devils: (Mark.3:14-15).*

Jesus is LORD

CHAPTER 2

Being a Faithful Husband Who Fulfills His Duties and Yields to His Wife's Needs and Desires 1st Corinthians 7:2-4

1. God instructs every husband to have his own wife and her only.

2. Letting go of mother's apron strings.

3. Placing friends and partners in their proper place.

4. Putting past lovers in their proper place.

5. Key points of being faithful to your wife.

6. The husband is to render to his wife due benevolence.

7. A husband's duties end where sin begins.

8. The key question: How well am I treating my wife?

9. The husband is to yield to his wife full control of his body.

…God's Divine Instructions To Husbands and Men

1. God instructs every husband to have his own wife and her only.

2. Nevertheless, to avoid fornication, let every man have his own wife. (1st Corinthians. 7:2)

During a man's life, he gains many close friends and partners in which he establishes many deep emotional bonds with; however, after he unites in marriage, the one person he should have the deepest and closest bond with is his wife. She is to be the most important person in his life, and no one is to be equal to her or more important than she is to him. Many men cause great stress and problems in their marriage because of three groups of people they hold equal to or higher than their wives. These three groups of people are (1) their mothers, (2) their partners and friends, and (3) their past lovers. They often put these people before their wives, and treat them with more respect than their wives. If a man desires to have a successful and fulfilling marriage, he must learn what it means to forsake all others, and to hold to his own wife by placing her above everyone else and everything else except God.

2. Letting go of mother's apron strings

Many men will not let go of their mothers' apron strings (nor do mothers let go of their sons); thus, it causes great problems for their wives and their marriage. A greater tragedy is that these men and mothers do not realize they are still holding on to each other. Husbands, you must realize when you are holding on to your mother, and then you must let go of that hold. You are holding on to your mother when after you and your wife has discussed something, you go and discuss it with your mother. You are holding on to your mother when you discuss every major decision with her, and you haven't discussed it with your wife. You are holding on when you discuss major decisions with your wife but then go and discuss it with your mother; and then take your mother's advice over your wife's.

Husbands, you must realize everything that goes on in your marriage is between you and your wife, and your mother should not be involved at all.

Don't discuss things with your mother when you and your wife have already settled it. If your mother is to be involved, let your wife consult her. You may feel that your mother is wiser than your wife and gives better advice, but you must realize that you and your wife are making a life together. You both will make mistakes, but you both must overcome them together.

Mothers, do not get involved in your son's marriage. Tell your son when he is mistreating his wife, but never get involved in their decision-making process. Whether they make good decisions or bad decisions, let the decisions be theirs to make. If you feel they are about to make a bad decision, talk to your daughter-in-law about it and not to your son; and then let your daughter-in-law know that regardless of what you say, she and her husband must make the final decision.

3. Placing friends and partners in their proper place

Another mistake a husband usually makes is to allow his friends and partners to come between him and his wife. He is usually with them when he should be with his wife. He is usually doing things with them when he should be doing things with his wife. He is usually doing things with them that he knows his wife does not approve of. Their drinking, cursing, horse-playing, staying out late, and other things of that nature are things a wife wishes her husband was not doing. He neglects her to be with them, and then takes the attitude that "These are my friends, and nobody comes before my friends."

Husbands, remember you vowed to forsake all others for her. Remember God wants you to have your own wife and to place her above all others. Although you have friends, they are never to come before your wife. You are never to neglect your wife because of them or for them; and if you are about to do anything with them that your wife won't approve of, you are not to do it. For this, your friends may call you henpecked, but God will call you a good husband. Also, a true friend is one who will never hinder your marriage but will do what he can to help make it better; even if making it better means not being with you as much and not doing the same things with you that he did before you were married.

4. Putting past lovers in their proper place

Before marriage, men were called players, lovers, and ladies' men. They were out to see how many ladies they could conquer, and how many ladies they could love. In the course of being a player and a ladies' man, some men may have developed some deep emotional relationships with certain women that are hard to break. Throughout the balance of their lives, they hold these "special ladies" close to their heart and refuse to break ties with them. Although the wife may not know of these relationships, yet these are relationships that must end.

Some men have children by women who are not their wives. Men, when you become the father to children whose mother is not your wife, you must remember that your relationship is with those children and not with their mother. Your interactions are to be with those children and not with their mother. You may discuss things with their mother that concerns them, but you are no longer to have a special or intimate relationship with her. She (nor any other woman that is not your wife) is never to hold a special place in your heart. Husbands, you must remember that God never tells you to hold on to past relationships and lovers; He tells you to have your own wife and her only.

5. Key points of being faithful to your wife

Someone once asked a wise old preacher how is it that he can be faithful to his wife and to her only. His answer was, "I am so busy looking at her only and loving her only that I do not have the time or the desire to look at or love any other woman." He said, "Beauty is in the eyes of the beholder, and she is all the beauty that my eyes want to behold." Faithfulness in marriage is something God demands, and God deals harshly with those who violate their marriage vows. Faithfulness is so important to God that he commands husbands to have their own wife and her only.

⁴And he answered and said unto them, Have ye not read, that he which made them at the beginning made them male and female, ⁵And said, For this cause shall a man leave father and mother, and shall cleave to his wife: and they twain shall be one flesh? ⁶Wherefore they are no more twain, but one flesh. What therefore God hath joined together, let not man put asunder. (Matthew.19:4-6)

To be faithful to your wife you must get so busy loving her that there is not enough room in your heart and life for any other woman

To be faithful to your wife, there are certain things you as a husband must do. First, you must get so busy loving her that there is not enough room in your heart and life for any other woman. Romance your wife when you need someone to romance, talk to her when you need someone to talk to, and do things with her when you need someone to do things with. Let your life be so filled with her and with your love for her that you won't have room nor time for any other woman.

To be faithful, never do anything with another woman you would not want another man doing with your wife.

Since you do not want another man flirting with your wife, do not flirt with another woman. Never take another woman out on a date (breakfast, lunch, or dinner); and never become close, personal, and intimate friends with another woman. These are things that you do not want your wife doing with another man, so do not do them with another woman. Following this rule will keep you from drawing closer than you should be with other woman, or another woman.

To be faithful to your wife, learn to love God so much that you will always strive to do what He says; even when He says to have your own wife and her only.

There may be times when you find your love and loyalty for your wife diminishing, and you will not be able to figure out why you should keep on loving her and being faithful to her. There will be times when you will meet other women and find yourself being drawn to them emotionally and sexually. And there will also be times when your wife will do things that will cause your love to decrease.

At such times as these, you must realize that the main reason to love your wife is because it is a command from the God whom you say you love. When things seem to be going wrong between you and your spouse, and when temptations are everywhere, you should be able to say to God, "I do not want to love my wife as I should, and I really want to yield to the temptations of the other woman, but, Lord, because I love you so much, I will obey you and love my wife as you have commanded. Lord, I will not yield to temptation." <u>Base your love and loyalty for your wife on your love and loyalty for your God, and when your love and loyalty for your God is right, you will always be faithful to your wife.</u>

6. The husband is to render to his wife due benevolence.

> [3.] *Let the husband render unto the wife due benevolence. (1st Corinthians.1: 7:3)*

One of the greatest problems confronting husbands today is not knowing what their role in marriage is and not fulfilling their role. God instructs a husband to render due benevolence to his wife. **Due benevolence** means rendering unto your wife all the duties and all of the good things that God instructs a husband to give to his wife. Not only does due benevolence include duties to perform and good things to give, it also includes the type of personality a husband is to possess. Husbands, it is your responsibility to learn what these due benevolences are, and then to learn to incorporate them into your marriage. Also, it is your responsibility to constantly improve in performing them.

To learn what duties to perform, good things to give, and personalities to possess, a husband must study the Word of God. He will also need to listen to sermons, talk to older godly men, and read books on the subject of what God instructs a husband to do. Throughout the course of this book, we will be discussing what due benevolences God requires of a husband as well as how to perform these due benevolences in one's marriage and life. God tells us that His people are destroyed because of a lack of knowledge.

6. **My people are destroyed for lack of knowledge**: *because thou hast rejected knowledge, I will also reject thee, that thou shalt be no priest to me: seeing thou hast forgotten the law of thy God, I will also forget thy children. (Hosea. 4:6)*

If you as a husband don't want you or your marriage to be destroyed, you must acquire the right knowledge and apply that knowledge into your life and marriage.

Once you begin seeking knowledge so you can obey God and start rendering due benevolence to your wife, God will give you the ability and power to perform such duties. As you read the Holy Bible and learn what God requires of you as a husband, you may feel you are unable to fulfill those requirements; however, you must realize that the Spirit of God is there to help you. To receive that help, make up your mind to be obedient to God and render to your wife the due benevolence He requires of you. This is not to be a one-time decision; it is to be a daily decision you must constantly remind yourself of.

After deciding to obey God, you must give yourself constantly to prayer. You are to pray that God will keep revealing to you what your duties are and that he will help you to perform them. You are to pray, asking God to deal with your wife in such ways that she will make it easy for you to render due benevolence unto her. You also must rely on the power of the Holy Ghost (who is in you if you are a Christian) to help you when you feel

you are unable to perform your duties. The Holy Ghost will strengthen you so you will be able to do that which you are supposed to do.

7. A husband's duties end where sin begins

When rendering due benevolence to your wife, you must remember that due benevolence does not require you to do anything sinful for her, to her, or with her. A husband's duties end where sin begins. God did not give her to you to cause you to do anything sinful. Husbands, it is very easy for you to love your wife so much that you will do everything you can for her, sometimes even sinful things. You can love her so much that you will do all you can to make her happy, even if making her happy means that you will have to do something God does not want you to do.

Adam loved Eve so much that he allowed her to cause him to sin.

6. And when the woman saw that the tree was good for food, and that it was pleasant to the eyes, and a tree to be desired to make one wise, she took of the fruit thereof, and did eat, and gave also unto her husband with her; and he did eat. (Genesis. 3:6)

Abraham loved Sarah so much that he allowed her to cause him to do something outside of God's will for them.

1 Now Sarai Abram's wife bare him no children: and she had an handmaid, an Egyptian, whose name was Hagar. 2 And Sarai said unto Abram, Behold now, the LORD hath restrained me from bearing: I pray thee, go in unto my maid; it may be that I may obtain children by her. And Abram hearkened to the voice of Sarai. (Genesis. 16:1-2)

Whenever you are tempted to sin to please your wife, always remember that the end result of a husband's sin is tragic. The whole human race is suffering because of a husband's (Adam) sin. Because of this husband's sin, sin entered into the world and was passed on to every generation. Adam was kicked out of paradise on earth (the Garden of Eden) because of a husband's (Adam) sin. The major enemy of the Jewish nation is a result of a husband's (Abraham) sin. The greatest problems that came into Abraham's home were because of a husband's (Abraham) sin.

Husbands, never sin to please your wife because sin causes great evils and sufferings to come on you, your wife, your family, and on others. Nothing good ever comes from a husband sinning to please his wife. The best thing and the wisest thing a husband can do in dealing with his wife is avoid sinning for her, or with her, and to treat her only the way God says to treat her.

8. The key question: How well am I treating my wife?

Every husband should constantly be asking himself how well he is treating his wife. He should be asking himself if he is doing all he can to treat her the way God commands. He should ask her how she feels about the way he treats her. If she tells him how to treat her better, he should be willing to do it. He should ask God to constantly teach him how to be a better husband and to lead him in his quest of seeking to become the kind of husband God instructs him to be.

Husbands, it takes much time, energy, and effort to become the kind of husband God wants you to be; and it is something you must constantly work at. You can never neglect your duties, and you must perform them even when your wife is not doing her part. It requires having a great imagination because, you will have to always be thinking of ways to make the marriage better and the wife happier.

It takes being good to your wife even when there seems to be no reason for being good. Remember your wife is a woman, and a woman likes women things. Women things includes being romantic, giving her compliments, giving her gifts for no special reason, and always showing her love, support, and respect. She needs to know that to you, she is of great worth and value and that the greatest love you hold in your heart (other than your love for Christ) is your love for her.

In order for any marriage to be a success, the husband must render due benevolence to his wife. When a husband fails to perform his duties, he sins against his wife, himself, and his God. When he fails to perform his duties, he is failing to fulfill the purpose that God intended him to fulfill as a husband. He is also failing to cause his marriage to fulfill the purpose God has for a

Christian marriage. That purpose is to make his marriage a reflection of how Christ treats His bride, the church.

³¹ For this cause shall a man leave his father and mother, and shall be joined unto his wife, and they two shall be one flesh. ³² This is a great mystery: but I speak concerning Christ and the church. (Ephesians.5:31-32)

Husbands, the responsibility of making your marriage a success rests more on you than on your wife. Make sure you are doing your part so your marriage will have a greater chance of being the success God wants it to be.

9. The husband is to yield to his wife full control of his body.

⁴· And likewise also the husband hath not power of his own body, but the wife. (1ˢᵗ Corinthians: 7:4)

While many men feel they have authority over their wives and that their wives must submit to them, they fail to realize that their wives have authority over them as well, and they too must submit to their wives. When a man unites in marriage to a woman, he yields full authority of his body over to her, according to the instructions of God. Everything he puts into his body, everywhere he goes with his body, and everything he does with his body must meet her approval. He is to do nothing that she does not want him to do. God does not only give authority and power to the man, but in certain areas, He also gives it to the woman. When it comes to a husband's body, that is an area where God has given the wife full authority.

The wife is to be able to control what her husband puts on his body that he has given her full authority over. She has the right to govern the type of clothes he wears, the type of cologne he wears, the style of his hair (how long, how short, and what style), the jewelry he wears, and all the things he may want to put on his body that he has yielded to her authority. She has the right to govern what he does with his body that he has given her authority over. She can tell him not to use his body for immorality, for fighting others, or for abusing himself in any way. Whatever he may want to do with his body, it must meet the approval of his wife because she has full control and authority over his body.

The wife has the right to govern what he puts into his body. She can tell him not to put into his body such things as drugs, alcohol, too much food, certain kinds of food, cigarette smoke, and whatever things she does not want in his body. The wife has the right to govern where he goes in his body that he has given her full authority over. She has the right to ask him not to go to nightclubs, gambling boats, and drug houses. She has the right to tell him not to go to certain people's homes or go any place where she does not approve of his body going.

A husband should never expect his wife to be submissive to him if he refuses to submit to her in the area of giving her full control and authority over his body. Most husbands like to be in authority over their wives but hate to be under their authority when it comes to their bodies. Husbands, if we want our wives to submit to us in other areas of life, we must learn to submit to them in this area of life. At times, we may not like submitting to our wives; but they, at times, hate submitting to our demands and requests also. Because they submit to us even if they do not want to, we too must submit to them at times when we do not want to.

While a wife has authority over her husband's body, the husband is still the head of the wife and family and has the highest authority (under Christ) in the home. Although the wife has authority over her husband's body, it does not relieve him of his responsibilities concerning the care of his family, as well as protecting them and setting the directions and goals of that home. He still has the responsibility for their spiritual and physical growth. He must approve of and be responsible for every major decision made at home. He is responsible for dealing with all problems, and he is the one to bring the family through all crises. The wife may control his body, but the husband is to control the family and home.

Father; only by the power and anointing of the Holy Ghost can husbands and men fulfill Your Divine instructions concerning them. Please keep them fill with the Holy Ghost, and please give them a heart of obedience. In Jesus' name I pray; amen.

[13] *For it is God which worketh in you both to will and to do of his good pleasure. (Philippians.2:13)*

[20] *Now the God of peace, that brought again from the dead our Lord Jesus, that great shepherd of the sheep, through the blood of the everlasting covenant,* [21] *Make you perfect in every good work to do his will, working in you that which is wellpleasing in his sight, through Jesus Christ; to whom be glory for ever and ever. Amen. (Hebrews.13:20-21).*

Jesus my LORD; because of Who you have place in us, men are well able to perform all You instruct us to do. Thank You for placing the greater One in me to strengthen me.

[13]*I can do all things through Christ which strengtheneth me. (Philippians.4:13).*

Jesus is LORD

Chapter 3

The Husband Is To Be His Wife's Lover and the Spiritual Head of His Family

1. The husband is to strive to have sexual fulfillment continually with his wife and with her only.

    A. Women's desires and needs change constantly.

    B. With women, sexual fulfillment is more mental and emotional than physical.

    C. Sex does not start in the bedroom.

    D. Men are excited by sight and touch while women are excited by romance and emotions.

    E. Men want sex all of the time while women want sex only some of the time.

    F. When your wife rejects sex, she is not rejecting you.

    G. The physical changes that occur in your wife's body affect her sexual desires and her mental attitude.

- H. As a woman gets older, her sexual drive decreases faster than her husband's.

- I. Husbands, never make sex in marriage the most important thing; make her and the family the most important things.

- J. Husbands, you will never be able to satisfy your wife fully if you do not pray and ask for God's help in that area.

2. Reasons why a wife can say no to sex with her husband.

3. The husband is to be a man of prayer and fasting.

4. Husbands are to teach their children the Word of God.

5. Husbands are to be men who studies and obeys the Word of God.

6. The husband is to do all he can to keep the devil from tempting his wife and family.

1. The husband is to strive to have sexual fulfillment continually with his wife and with her only.

5. ***Defraud ye not one the other,*** *except it be with consent for a time, that ye may give yourselves to fasting and prayer; and come together again, that the devil tempt you not for your incontinency.* (1st Corinthians. 7:5)

Sex in marriage is an enriching and fulfilling experience ordained by God to be enjoyed as often as desired between the husband and wife. God instructs married couples, in His Word, not to defraud or deprive each other of such an experience. A married couple can abstain from sexual fulfillment if both agree, but they are to come together again very soon so that the devil will not be able to tempt them because of their incontinency (lack of self-control in the matter of sensuous desires). To defraud or deprive each other sexually can occur in two forms: (1) when one spouse refuses to have sexual relations with his or her spouse for non-biblical reasons, and (2) when one spouse engages in sexual relations with his or her spouse but does not do it to the fullness of his or her ability.

When it comes to sexual fulfillment in marriage, men think they know all there is to know, when in reality, there is much he needs to learn. If a husband is going to strive to cause his wife to reach her sexual fullness, he must come to the realization that it will be a learning process for him that will last a lifetime. He will be constantly learning what to do (because she changes so often), when to do it, where lovemaking begins, and how to do what needs to be done when it's time to do it.

He will also need to learn that what works for other women will not necessarily work for his wife. He must learn her likes and dislikes, what she wants and what she does not want, and when and where are the best times and places for her. He must learn that he can't do the same things every time because this will not always please her. Sexual fulfillment in marriage is a lifetime learning course that a husband needs to take, and it is a course he cannot afford to fail.

While all women and men are not always the same, there are some important facts husbands need to know about women, about sex in marriage, and about his wife if he is going to fulfill his wife's needs and desires sexually and keep the instruction of God not to defraud his wife.

A. Women's desires and needs change constantly.

Husbands, you will find that the things you do now to please your wife will one day no longer please her. Her desires and needs change, and you must be constantly seeking to learn when these changes occur and what changes you must make in order to give her sensuous satisfaction. What worked yesterday will not necessarily work today. One of the major mistakes a man makes is falling into a sexual routine with his wife and not noticing that she is not being satisfied. Husbands, notice your wife's changes, and then change with her.

B. With women, sexual fulfillment is more mental and emotional than physical.

While a woman can enjoy sex with a man whom she does not love, she will only reach her highest sexual fulfillment with the man she does love (i.e., if that man is her husband). If you, as a husband, expect to totally satisfy your wife, your number one job is to make sure she loves you with all of her heart. You should constantly do things to keep her love alive and growing. If she stops loving you, she will also stop being fulfilled by you. Women will stay married for love even if the sex is not very good, but women will not stay married just for good sex, if the love is gone. They will stay for love, but they will not stay just for sex.

When a wife loves her husband but there is contention between them, she usually does not want intimacy; and if she does it anyway, she will not enjoy it to the fullest. Husbands, you must protect the heart and mind of your wife if you want to please her. Find ways to put her at ease, make her feel secure, and surround her with your love. Do all you can to avoid creating contention; and when contentions do occur, seek to make it short, and end it with apologies and words of love. Do something special for her to ease her mind and put her heart at rest. Doing these things will help her realize that even when contentions occur, you still love her, and doing these things will also help bring fulfillment when it's time to make love to her.

C. Sex does not start in the bedroom.

As soon as a man gets into the bedroom, he is ready for lovemaking. If his wife is not ready before she gets into the bedroom, it will be hard for her to get ready upon entering the room. Husbands, start at the beginning of the day getting your wife ready for the end of the day. Hugs and kisses throughout the day help get her ready for the end of the day. Helping around the house (with dishes, housework, and kids) during the day, helps get her ready for the end of the day. Dinners out and romantic escapades during the day help get her ready for the end of the day. A failure at the end of a day in the bedroom, is really a result of a failure that occurred at the beginning of the day and throughout the day.

D. Men are excited by sight and touch while women are excited by romance and emotions.

Husbands, if you take romance out of your marriage, you will also take sexual fulfillment out of your marriage. Women are creatures of romance and of the delicate things of life. Wine and roses, dinner and dancing, soft lights, and romantic music are all parts of her makeup. Give her those things, and they will excite her into ecstasy; deny her those things, and sex will be an unfulfilling experience that she does not look forward to.

Husbands, remember that what romance is to one woman may be different from what romance is to another. While evenings out may be romantic to one woman, to another, romance is being at home watching television while being held by her husband. Find out what is romantic to your wife, and then do those things for her.

God's Divine Instructions To Husbands and Men

E. Men want sex all of the time while women want sex only some of the time.

A husband must realize that his sex drive is higher and greater than his wife's, and while he is always in the mood for love, his wife is not. He must try to understand that, and then he must give his wife the freedom of "not feeling like it tonight." She does not have to be tired, sick, nor on her cycle; it may be just one of those occasions when she does not feel like being intimate. When that time comes, husbands, it is not the time to exercise anger; it is time to exercise self-discipline, understanding, and loving patience.

F. When your wife rejects sex, she is not rejecting you.

To a husband, sex in marriage is a part of him, a part of his love, and a part of the way he shows love. When his wife rejects making love to him, he feels that she is rejecting him, his love, and his way of showing love. Women know how to love and receive love even when there is no sex involved. Women know that a person can experience love and show love without engaging in sex. Husbands feel that sex and love is like wet and water; you can't have one without the other. To reject the wet is to reject the water, and to reject the sex is to reject his love, and to reject one of the ways he shows love.

We as husbands must realize that just as we love our wives when we are not being intimate with them, they love us when they are not being intimate with us. When they reject sex with us, they are not rejecting us; they are just being true to their nature of not desiring sexual intimacy as much as men. We as husbands must realize that sex is not the wife's first and major priority in marriage. Women are creatures of love and affection, and they know how to show that love and affection even when sex is not a part of it.

G. The physical changes that occur in your wife's body affect her sexual desires and her mental attitude.

PMS and menopause are physical changes wives go through that often cause them to not desire intimacy, and these conditions also cause them to react in ways that are not so pleasant. These are powerful changes they are dealing with, and because we do not experience them, we cannot understand what our wives are going through. When our wives go through these changes, we as husbands must remember all of the times they have shown nothing but love and respect for us, and then we must give them the grace and the support they need while going through these powerful changes. It isn't that they don't truly love us, and they are not really trying to disrespect us. They are just dealing with some hard physical and mental changes. When we show them love, patience, and understanding during their times of change, they may show us great fulfillment during the times they are not going through those powerful changes.

H. As a woman gets older, her sexual drive decreases faster than her husband's.

Men, she can't handle it like she used to, so don't ask her to. Also, husbands, remember and realize that you ain't all you used to be either. You are getting older, and so is she. Age affects men and women in different ways. As we get older, our bellies stick out, and their desires decrease. (Sometimes I wonder if the way we look when we are in our underwear have anything to do with their desires decreasing.)

Husbands, it is just a rule of nature that as women mature, their desires decrease faster than ours. As we get older, we must be able to exercise greater self-control. Let us exercise that control when it comes to our wives' decreasing desires. We may not engage in sex as much, but when we do, seek to make it more intimate and fulfilling. This will bring a greater joy to the marriage and will cause you and your spouse to remain close. It will also cause you and her to feel as if you all are still united as one. A lack of sexual contact can cause division in a marriage; but self-control, understanding, and communication can keep that division from occurring.

I. Husbands, never make sex in marriage the most important thing; make her and the family the most important things.

Husbands, your wife needs to know that if something happens to her and she could not engage in sex with you, (1) you will not stop loving her, (2) you will not leave her, and (3) you will not turn to another woman seeking sexual fulfillment. Always reassure your wife that while you like sex, you love her. Let her know that she is the only woman you want to make love to, and you will never leave her because she can't make love to you. Tell her that you will not turn to someone else for sex because it is not sex you love; it is having sex with her that you love and desire.

J. Husbands, you will never be able to satisfy your wife fully if you do not pray and ask for God's help in that area.

God is the author of sex, and He is the one who designed it for marriage. It is He who will teach you what you need to know about sex in marriage, and it is He who will give you the power and ability to perform to the fullest you can. Don't be embarrassed to pray about that area of marriage because it is an area ordained of God.

2. Reasons why a wife can say no to sex with her husband.

While it is God's will for a couple to engage in sexual fulfillment regularly, and he tells each spouse not to defraud their spouse, there are times when God allows a spouse to refuse having sex with their partner. If your wife is sick, or if she is on her menstruation period, she can refuse you. Husbands, when your wife is physically tired, that should be a sufficient and acceptable reason for her to refuse you sexual fulfillment without you getting upset. Another reason for a wife and her husband not to have sex together is if both agree to abstain for a short while, so that they may give themselves to prayer and fasting.

Whenever a couple abstains from sexual fulfillment for any reason, God wants those times to be short and few. God knows that when a couple refrains from sexual fulfillment with one another, the devil will come in and try to tempt one or both to seek sexual fulfillment outside the home. In order to combat such temptations of the devil, God puts a limit on the reasons one spouse can deny the other, and then commands them to return to sexual relations quickly.

3. The husband is to be a man of prayer and fasting.

*5. Defraud ye not one the other, except it be with consent for a time, **that ye may give yourselves to fasting and prayer**; and come together again, that the devil tempt you not for your incontinency. (1ˢᵗ Corinthians. 7:5)*

A major reason many marriages fail or never reach the fullness it ought to reach is because of the failure of the husband to be the spiritual head of his family. Many men do well as the provider and protector of their families, but they totally neglect being the spiritual leader. Husbands, being the spiritual leader of your family should be so important to you, that you should be willing to give up sex for a short while in order to give yourself to prayer and fasting. Husbands, you will never be called a successful and good "head of the family" by God when you fail to be their spiritual leader.

Certain things are required of you as a husband if you are to become the spiritual head of your family. These requirements include; (1) being saved, (2) being a man of prayer and fasting, (3) being a man who studies and obeys the Word of God, (4) being more spiritually inclined than your wife so that you may be able to answer her spiritual questions, and (5) being a man who teaches your children the Word and the ways of God. If you as a husband are not fulfilling those minimal requirements, you are failing miserably as a spiritual head of your family.

According to the Word of God, every Christian husband should be a man of prayer and fasting. If you are a husband, prayer should be a major part of your life. You should have realized by now that you need God's help in leading your family. You need God to provide, protect, and bless your family. You need Him to guide the family in the right ways and to keep the marriage together and fulfilling. You also need God to bless your children to grow up to be all He wants them to be. For all this to happen in your life, you will need much prayer, fasting, and faith.

Husbands, it is your responsibility to make sure that you are a man of prayer, and it's your responsibility to teach your family to pray. You are to be the one who calls the family together for daily prayer. Your family needs to learn how to pray, and they are to learn by seeing and hearing you pray consistently. Oftentimes, it is the wife who teaches the children to pray, and she is usually the one who prays with them. Yet, husbands, God intended for you to take that role and responsibility.

4. And, ye fathers, provoke not your children to wrath: but bring them up in the nurture and admonition of the Lord. (Ephesians.6:4)

As a man of prayer, you must add fasting with your prayers once in a while. To fast means to deny yourself certain important physical needs and desires in order to care for spiritual needs. You may deny yourself such things as food, friends, entertainment, sex, and other earthly things in order to seek God in prayer and fasting. Fasting is one of the most powerful things you can do spiritually to remove and keep the devil and his demons out of your family and life.

25 When Jesus saw that the people came running together, he rebuked the foul spirit, saying unto him, Thou dumb and deaf spirit, I charge thee, come out of him, and enter no more into him. 26 And the spirit cried, and rent him sore, and came out of him: and he was as one dead; insomuch that many said, He is dead. 27 But Jesus took him by the hand, and lifted him up; and he arose. 28 And when he was come into the house, his disciples asked him privately, Why could not we cast him out? 29 And he said unto them, This kind can come forth by nothing, but by prayer and fasting. (Mark 9:25-29)

4. Husbands are to be men who studies and obeys the Word of God.

To be a good spiritual head of your home, you must be a person who studies and obeys the Word of God daily. To study and obey the Word will enable you and your family to stand when rough times arrive.

²⁴· Therefore whosoever heareth these sayings of mine, and doeth them, I will liken him unto a wise man, which built his house upon a rock: ²⁵ And the rain descended, and the fl oods came, and the winds blew, and beat upon that house; and it fell not: for it was founded upon a rock. (Matthew. 7:24-25)

Studying and obeying the Word of God will also cause you to prosper and have good success in life.

⁸ This book of the law shall not depart out of thy mouth; but thou shalt meditate therein day and night, that thou mayest observe to do according to all that is written therein: **_for then thou shalt make thy way prosperous, and then thou shalt have good success_**. *(Joshua.1:8)*

It will also cause you to grow in the grace and knowledge of our Lord and Savior Jesus Christ.

¹⁸ **_But grow in grace, and in the knowledge of our Lord and Saviour Jesus Christ._** *To him be glory both now and for ever. Amen. (2ⁿᵈ Peter. 3:18)*

In the eyes of God, no husband can be called a good husband if he does not study and obey the Word of God.

To be a good spiritual head of your family, you must be as spiritually inclined as your wife, or even more. If your wife has any questions about something she hears in church, she is to come and ask you at home about it.

³⁴ Let your women keep silence in the churches: for it is not permitted unto them to speak; but they are commanded to be under obedience, as also saith the law. ³⁵And if they will learn any thing, let them ask their husbands at home: for it is a shame for women to speak in the church. (1st Corinthians. 14:34-35)

God placed the man as the head of the wife and family. This headship position not only includes leading the family physically, but it also includes leading the family spiritually. Usually, the wife knows more about the Holy Bible than the husband. This happens because (1) she spends more time reading and studying it, and (2) she spends more time in church than her husband. Husbands, you must increase your study time, and you must also spend more time in church so that you can become more spiritually advanced than you are now. You are not competing against your wife; you are just seeking to be the spiritually mature Christian and husband that God desires you to be.

5. Husbands are to teach their children the Word of God.

It is the duty of the husband, along with his wife, to teach the children the Word of God and the things of God. The wife is to be the main teacher of the Word of God to the children only when her husband fails to do so. God tells fathers to bring the children up in the nurture and admonition of the Lord.

⁴ And, ye fathers, provoke not your children to wrath: but bring them up in the nurture and admonition of the Lord. (Ephesians.6:4)

God tells the fathers that in everything they do, and at all times, they are to tell their children about the wonderful things of God.

⁷· And thou shalt teach them diligently unto thy children, and shalt talk of them when thou sittest in thine house, and when thou walkest by the way, and when thou liest down, and when thou risest up. (Deuteronomy.6:7)

Husbands, the most important thing you can do in this life is to lead your wife and children toward salvation. You cannot ensure they will be saved, but you can teach them the Word of God and introduce them to Jesus Christ. You can pray for them, take them to church, and live the Christian life before them. These are things you can do to try to get them saved. If you raise your child to become the president of this country or to rise to some other prominent earthly position, and then they die and spend an eternity in the lake of fire, if you did not try to get them saved, you have failed as a husband and as a father.

The duties and responsibilities of a husband and a father are so great that God knew he would need much prayer and fasting. One of the strongest needs and desires a man has is his need and desire for sexual fulfillment. Husbands, God want your need and desire for prayer and fasting to exceed your need and desire for sex. If, to you, sex is more important than prayer, your priorities are confused; and you must make changes. Prayer and fasting is more than just a need that a man should fulfill; it is a command from God that a man should obey.

6. The husband is to do all he can to keep the devil from tempting his wife and family.

*5. Defraud ye not one the other, except it be with consent for a time, that ye may give yourselves to fasting and prayer; and come together again, **that the devil tempt you not** for your incontinency. (1st Corinthians. 7:5)*

The husband should stand as a watchman over the family to guard and protect it against the temptations and attacks of the devil. The devil is as "a roaring lion seeking whom he may devour," and we as husbands have the charge of standing against him when he seeks to devour our wives and children. We, husbands, stand against him as we fulfill our duty of being the spiritual head of our homes by praying for our family, by teaching them the Word of God, by taking them to church, and by being a Christian example for them. We are not to tolerate any sinful behavior in our home; and if someone sins, we are to deal with it quickly, firmly, and in a Christ-like manner.

Husbands, before the devil can destroy your home, he must first bind you.

²⁹ Or else how can one enter into a strong man's house, and spoil his goods, except he first bind the strong man? and then he will spoil his house. (Matthew.12:29)

The devil tries to binds you by; (1) causing you to neglect fulfilling your spiritual responsibilities in the home, (2) causing you to distrust God by no longer trusting in His Word, and (3) causing you to get caught up into continual sin. Husbands, guard yourself first (by immersing yourself in God), and then you will be able to guard your family.

The husband is to do all he can to keep his wife and family from sinning; if they sin, it is their fault, and they must bear the responsibility for it. If you have taught them right from wrong, and they choose the wrong, it is their fault; and they cannot blame it on you, on others, or on the devil. The ultimate responsibility to turn down sin and temptation is theirs. Should you as a husband see that your wife or children are headed down the pathway of sin, you are to warn them and to do what you can to stop them. You are to seek to do all you can to turn them away from sinful behavior; however, the ultimate responsibility to refrain from committing sin is theirs.

Husbands, while it is the wife's ultimate responsibility to turn down sin and temptation, there are things you can do to help keep her from being tempted. You are to do your best to fulfill her physical and emotional needs so she will not have to sin to get them met. You are to fulfill her sexual and romantic needs so she won't have to seek for someone else to do it. Talk with her, and be the one with whom she can talk to when she needs conversation. If she talks more on the telephone than she talks to you, that may be a sign to you that she may need more conversation from you. Husbands, never let it be truthfully said by your wife that you never talk nor listen to her.

Husbands, strive to be your wife's best friend. Seek to be the one whom she enjoys being with the most. Do things with her, go places with her, and seek ways to be the one who brings her, her greatest joys and laughter. You cannot be everything to her that she needs and wants (no one can do or be that but God), but you can be all that she will allow you to be, and all that she reasonably expects you to be. While the devil is always seeking to tempt your wife and family, you should always be there to stop him and to try to take away every avenue he would try to use to induce them into sin.

Husbands, you must never get involved in any sin that your wife is doing, and you must turn down any sinful temptations she brings your way. Husbands, it is your responsibility to stand firm and to tell your wife not to commit sin. Oftentimes, when you ask your wife not to do something that she wants to do, it causes great conflict between you and her. Regardless of how great the conflict is; you must stand on what you believe is right in the eyes of God.

Jesus is LORD

CHAPTER 4

Holding On to and Sanctifying Your Wife

1. The husband is never to put away his wife.

2. The devil will try to give you reasons why you should leave your wife.

3. The devil will also try to get you to do things to cause the marriage to end.

4. The devil will also try to cause contention in your marriage so you or your wife will react in wrong ways.

5. The devil will try to keep you from knowing what your duties are, and from performing those duties.

6. The husband is to live in such ways that God will sanctify his wife.

1. The husband is to never put away his wife.

¹¹· But and if she depart, let her remain unmarried or be reconciled to her husband: and let not the husband put away his wife. (1ˢᵗ Corinthians. 7:11)

A major lesson that you as a husband need to learn is that your marriage is to represent the relationship Jesus Christ has with His bride, the church. All that you do concerning your marriage should be geared toward that purpose (representing Christ and His church). Love your wife as Christ loves His church, cherish your wife as Christ cherishes His church, and treat your wife as Christ treats His church. Jesus Christ will never put away His bride, the church; so, husbands, never put your wife away.

God wants your marriage to last a lifetime, and He wants to work through you to cause that to happen. the devil is doing everything he can to try to destroy your marriage; and he will always (1) try to give you reasons to leave your wife, (2) try to get you to do things that will cause your marriage to end, and (3) try to keep you from doing the things necessary to keep the marriage together. Husbands, you are to be the one God is using to try to keep the marriage together. Never be the one the devil is using to try to destroy the marriage.

2. The devil will try to give you reasons why you should leave your wife.

After you have been married a while, the devil will tell you that, joy, happiness, and love are gone from your marriage. He will tell you that you and your wife have grown apart and will never come back together. He will tell you that you need to be happy, but as long as you are with her, you will never be happy. Because of these reasons, he will tell you, you should leave and start a new and better life without your wife.

Husbands, when you begin to entertain thoughts of that nature, you must recognize they come from the devil and then cast them down. When problems come into the marriage, it is not time for you to entertain thoughts of leaving, but it is time for you to seek God for solutions. Work to bring back into your marriage joy, happiness, and love. Work to do things that will cause you and your wife to grow back together. Never entertain ideas of leaving; entertain ideas of how to make the marriage last and get better.

If joy, happiness, and love are gone from your marriage, there are certain things you can do to try to restore them. You should begin with fasting and prayer, thus seeking God's intervention into the marriage. Next, try to develop things you and your wife can do together. These things can be as simple as washing dishes together, doing housework together, and doing yard work together. Schedule times when you and she can go places and spend quality time together. Seek to find out things she likes to do and begin doing them with her and for her.

3. The devil will also try to get you to do things to cause the marriage to end.

The devil will have you neglect your wife, family, home, and other responsibilities. He will try to cause you to treat her in a mean and harsh way. The devil will try to keep you from treating your wife as God says to treat her. He will even cause you to meet other women whom you may be attracted to so he can use them to destroy your marriage. Anything that happens in your marriage that tries to destroy it, is the work of the devil.

Never allow the devil to use you in any way to destroy your marriage. Instead of being used of the devil to destroy your marriage, be use of God to strengthen and develop your marriage.

4. The devil will also try to cause contention in your marriage so you or your wife will react in wrong ways.

The devil is hoping that contentions in your marriage, which lead to wrong reactions, will eventually cause the destruction of your marriage. Husbands, beware of arguments and how you handle them. You can be angry, but you are never to sin, and never let the sun go down on your wrath. You should be the one to find a peaceful solution to problems. Learn to talk to your wife gently and try to understand her viewpoints. Never allow anger and contentions to destroy your marriage; overcome anger and contentions, and then use them to make the marriage better and stronger.

5. The devil will try to keep you from knowing what your duties are, and from performing those duties.

There are certain duties and responsibilities that God tells a husband to perform for his wife. Not knowing what God says to do, and not doing what God says to do, will result in your marriage not being as fulfilling as it should be, and it may eventually cause the destruction of your marriage. Husbands, learn what your part in marriage is, and make it your priority to do it. Doing your part in marriage will keep you from being the cause of your marriage breaking up, and being destroyed by the devil.

While it is God's desire for a marriage to last a lifetime, there are certain reasons that God will allow the couple to separate. While they are apart, God wants them to work on solving their problems and work on getting back together. God hates divorces and separations.

15 And did not he make one? Yet had he the residue of the spirit. And wherefore one? That he might seek a godly seed. Therefore take heed to your spirit, and let none deal treacherously against the wife of his youth. 16. **For the LORD, the God of Israel, saith that he hateth putting away:** *for one covereth violence with his garment, saith the LORD of hosts: therefore take heed to your spirit, that ye deal not treacherously. (Malachi. 2:15-16)*

<u>God's ultimate goal for marriage is for the marriage to be a reflection of Christ and His church, and for the marriage to last until the death of one of the spouses.</u> If there is adultery, abuse, or abandonment, God will allow for separation and eventually, divorce. If your wife commits adultery and refuses to repent of that sin, you as her husband can separate from her and eventually divorce her. If she is willing to totally repent and be faithful to you, God

wants you to forgive her and get back together with her. There will be strong emotions and hurts to overcome. She may have to work hard at regaining your trust, and you will have to work hard at trying to trust her again.

If you refuse to remain with your wife because she has committed adultery, and you seek a divorce, God will not hold that against you. However, you need to remember the many times you committed spiritual adultery against Jesus (you are married to Christ) and needed His forgiveness. Whenever you sin in any manner, you are making love to the devil and thus committing spiritual adultery against your spiritual husband Jesus Christ. Jesus did not divorce you nor did He put you away; He forgave you and restored you. Husbands, forgive your wife, and restore her and your marriage.

[25] **_And when ye stand praying, forgive,_** *if ye have ought against any: that your Father also which is in heaven may forgive you your trespasses.* [26] **_But if ye do not forgive, neither will your Father which is in heaven forgive your trespasses._** *(Mark 11:25-26)*

Restoration of a marriage after there has been adultery is often a difficult thing to do. The hurts and mistrust run deep into the soul. Within your own power, it is hard to forgive. Start off by asking God to give you the power to forgive your wife. Next, begin forgiving her by faith. To forgive by faith, you must start by saying you forgive her even when in your heart you do not feel like you really have. We walk by faith and not by feelings. You are to work to bring your feelings under the control of your faith. Saying it will not be easy, but you have to say it. Say it to yourself, say it to your God, and say it to your wife.

To forgive after committing adultery will also require much work and maybe much counseling. It will also require much time because only God and time can heal the deep emotional hurt that you feel. You will both need to seek spiritual counseling from your pastor or from a professional Christian counselor. Much prayer will also be needed. You will need to pray alone as well as pray with your wife.

If your wife physically or mentally abuses you and your children, you may separate from her (for you and your children's sake). While separated, you are to seek professional mental and spiritual counseling for her. Once she is over her problem, you and she may get back together.

If your wife abandons you, you may, if she refuses to return, seek a divorce. If she forces you to leave and it is no fault of yours, you may leave and seek a divorce if she refuses to allow you to come back. However, before seeking the divorce, seek to find ways of reconciliation. If reconciliation seems impossible you may divorce.

If you as a husband feel that you must divorce your wife, make sure it is for biblical reasons only and because your wife refuses to repent of her sins and wrongdoings. Don't be a contributing factor toward her sinning by not doing the things you are supposed to do for her as her husband. If you divorce for the right reasons, God will forgive you, and you are free to marry another but only in the Lord (i.e., another Christian).

When trouble comes into a marriage, there will be times when you will feel you should not be the one to try to make the marriage work. You may feel that if your wife wants things to get better, she should be the one to try to make them better. Husbands, you are to be the head of the marriage; and if things are to get better (and stay better), you are to be the one who must begin making them better. You must remember Jesus began reaching out to you long before you reached for Him. You must reach out to your wife long before she begins reaching out to you.

There will also be times when your wife will not be doing her part as a wife; and you may want to separate, and/or get a divorce; or be unfaithful. During such times as these, you must continue doing your part even when she is not doing hers. You must remember God never promised that if you do your part, she would do her part also. You do your part not because you think she will respond by loving you; you do your part only because God tells you to. You are doing it for God and not for yourself nor for your wife.

I believe that if you do your part in marriage, your wife will eventually begin doing her part. It may take much patience to continue, but you must exercise patience, and you must continue. When you do your part, God will begin working on the heart of your wife to try and get her to begin doing her part as a wife. If, after doing your part, she still refuses to fulfill her part, take pleasure in knowing God is well pleased with you as a husband.

When it comes to divorce and separation, every husband must remember that God hates it. Never seek a separation or divorce until after you have done all you can to try to restore the marriage, and after you have done all you can to try to make the marriage better. Husbands, always keep in mind that God instructs you never to put your wife away.

6. The husband is to live in such ways that God will sanctify his wife.

[14] *For the unbelieving husband is sanctified by the wife, and **the unbelieving wife is sanctified by the husband:** else were your children unclean; but now are they holy. (1st Corinthians.7:14)*

One of the most important things a husband can do is to give his heart and life to Jesus Christ for salvation. There are many benefits to being a Christian, and one such benefit is that God will sanctify a Christian husband's wife for his sake, and for his children's sake (if his wife is a Christian already, she is sanctified because she is saved). God so wants He blessings and protection to be in a home that H will provide them even if there is just one person in the home that is a Christian. For the unbelieving wife to be sanctified by her husband does not mean she is automatically saved. It means that although she is still a sinner and is on her way to hell, God will set her aside for blessings and protection because she is married to one of His sons. A saved husband adds great spiritual blessings to his family because he has God involved in his family to bless him, his wife, and his children.

It is important for you as a husband (1) to be saved, (2) to know you are saved, and (3) to live the saved lifestyle. If you want to become a Christian, you must be ready to repent of your sins, and of the devil; and turn to righteousness through Jesus Christ. You must believe that Jesus Christ is the only begotten son of God who died on the cross for the sins of the world and that three days later, God raised Him from the dead. Next, you must confess with your mouth that you want Jesus Christ to forgive you of your sins, come into your heart, and be the Lord and Savior of your life.

9 That if thou shalt confess with thy mouth the Lord Jesus, and shalt believe in thine heart that God hath raised him from the dead, thou shalt be saved. 10 For with the heart man believeth unto righteousness; and with the mouth confession is made unto salvation. 11 For the scripture saith, Whosoever believeth on him shall not be ashamed. 12 For there is no difference between the Jew and the Greek: for the same Lord over all is rich unto all that call upon him. 13 For whosoever shall call upon the name of the Lord shall be saved. (Romans. 10:9-13)

After becoming a Christian, you need to be sure of your salvation (you need to know for a fact that you are saved). To know that you are saved, ask yourself two questions: (1) Have you done what God said to do to become a Christian? (2) Are you living the kind of lifestyle God says a Christian should live?

Has there ever been a time when you called upon (asked) Jesus Christ to be the Lord and Savior of your life? Many people have joined a church, but they have never asked Jesus to save them nor have they asked Him to come and live within their hearts. They have never given their life to Jesus so that He could become their Lord. To be Lord means that Jesus has the right to control every area of your life. It means that you and your life no longer belong to you; they now belong to Jesus. After you have repented, believed in Jesus, and have asked Him to be your Lord and Savior, you are saved, and you can know it (i.e., you can be assured of your salvation).

*[13] These things have I written unto you that believe on the name of the Son of God; **that ye may know that ye have eternal life,** and that ye may believe on the name of the Son of God. (1st John. 5:13)*

After doing what God says to do to become a Christian, you can know you are saved because you live the Christian lifestyle. It is impossible to have the kind of belief in Jesus that brings salvation and still live a sinful lifestyle.

[16] Know ye not, that to whom ye yield yourselves servants to obey, his servants ye are to whom ye obey; whether of sin unto death, or of obedience unto righteousness? (Romans. 6:16)

[44] Ye are of your father the devil, and the lusts of your father ye will do. He was a murderer from the beginning, and abode not in the truth, because there is no truth in him. When he speaketh a lie, he speaketh of his own: for he is a liar, and the father of it. (John 8:44).

Many people are like demons; they believe and tremble, but they are not saved.

[19] Thou believest that there is one God; thou doest well: the devils also believe, and tremble. (James 2:19).

Many people say they believe in Jesus and that He died and rose again, but they never gave Him their hearts and lives for salvation. Thus, they were never saved. Believing is good, but it's not enough. It takes the kind of believing and confessing (asking to be saved) that leads to a changed lifestyle. Many people are deceived into thinking they are Christians when they are not. If you are living a sinful lifestyle and think you are saved, you are deceived, and you need to examine yourself.

[5] **_Examine yourselves, whether ye be in the faith; prove your own selves. Know ye not your own selves, how that Jesus Christ is in you, except ye be reprobates?_** *(2nd Corinthians 13:5)*

God tells us that no person living in unrighteousness shall inherit is kingdom. He tells us not to be deceived into thinking we can.

[9] **_Know ye not that the unrighteous shall not inherit the kingdom of God? Be not deceived: neither fornicators, nor idolaters, nor adulterers, nor effeminate, nor abusers of themselves with mankind, 10 Nor thieves, nor_**

covetous, nor drunkards, nor revilers, nor extortioners, shall inherit the kingdom of God. *(1ˢᵗ Corinthians. 6:9-10)*

¹⁹ Now the works of the flesh are manifest, which are these; Adultery, fornication, uncleanness, lasciviousness, ²⁰ Idolatry, witchcraft, hatred, variance, emulations, wrath, strife, seditions, heresies, ²¹Envyings, murders, drunkenness, revellings, and such like: of the which I tell you before, as I have also told you in time past, ***that they which do such things shall not inherit the kingdom of God.*** *(Galatians. 5:19-21)*

To know for a fact you are a Christian, do what it takes to get saved, and then seek to live the kind of lifestyle a Christian should live.

To live a Christian lifestyle does not mean you will never sin again. It does not mean you will not be caught up into a season of sin. To live a Christian lifestyle means you are seeking to live as God's Word says. When you sin, you will confess it to God, repent of it, and then seek to continue living as God says to live in His Word. There may be many times when you stumble and fall into sin, but you will not lie there in the sin; you will get up (repent), dust yourself off (confess), and start walking again toward where you wanted to go (start living the type of life God says to live). Confession, repentance, and restoration are always a major part of living the Christian lifestyle.

While confession, repentance, and restoration are parts of the Christian life as we grow in Christ, we should find that our confession of sin, repentance of sin, and restoration because we have sinned should happen less and less, while our ability to live as God says should increase more and more. Adults fall less than children, children fall less than toddlers, and toddlers fall less than babies who are just starting to try to walk. The more they grow, the less they fall. As a saint, the more you grow, the less you should be falling into sin. Do not let a sin you've committed cause you to think you are not saved, but if there is continual sin in your life, you need to check yourself and your salvation.

Although God will sanctify your wife for your sake, she will eventually die and go to hell unless she gives her heart and life to Jesus Christ for salvation.

She may fall into the trap of thinking all is well for her because things are going good in her life. Let her know it is because of you being saved that things are going well for her, but she is still lost and is in need of Jesus for herself. She can ride on your blessings in this life, but they will not carry her into eternity.

Father; I want to be an example that You can use to show husbands and men what You desire them to be. Thank You for daily and constantly transforming me more and more into what You instructs us to be. I refuse to rebel against and fight against what You are seeking to do in me. In Jesus' name I pray; amen.

[12]*Let no man despise thy youth; but be thou an example of the believers, in word, in conversation, in charity, in spirit, in faith, in purity. (1st Timothy.4:12).*

Jesus my LORD; You are the great bridegroom. I must, by the power of the Holy Ghost, pattern myself and my life after the example of You; so I may be an example to others to Your glory.

Jesus is LORD

CHAPTER 5

Husbands Living Right for Their Children and Seeking to Please Their Wives

1. The husband is to live in such ways that his children will be clean and holy.

2. The husband is to please his wife.

3. My personal quest of trying to please my wife

4. The husband is to remember that he and his wife are bound together for life.

God's Divine Instructions To Husbands and Men

1. The husband is to live in such ways that his children will be clean and holy.

$^{44.}$ For the unbelieving husband is sanctified by the wife, and the unbelieving wife is sanctified by the husband: else were your children unclean; but now are they holy. (1st Corinthians. 7:14)

Not only does a saved husband cause his wife to be sanctified by God, he also causes God to consider his children as clean and holy. Being considered by God as clean and holy does not mean they are considered saved. To be clean and holy means that although they are still sinners, God will treat them and bless them like He would if they were Christians. However, for them to become Christians, they too must accept Jesus Christ as their personal Lord and Savior. Until they accept Jesus, the righteousness of the saved parent will cover them.

When the children of a saved parent reach an age where they can be accountable for their own actions and choices, God no longer deals with them through their parents' righteousness. God begins to deal with them through their own level of understanding righteousness and their choices to receive it or reject it. Knowing that one day your children will have to deal with God for themselves should cause you to live the Christian lifestyle in their presence and to do all you can to seek their salvation.

What are you doing to seek the salvation of your children? Are you praying for them every day and night? Do you take them to church and Bible study? Are you teaching them the Word of God in your home? Most important of all, are you saved and living the Christian lifestyle before them? Do they see Christian love and holiness in you? Do you tell them why you are saved and why you do the things you do? The eternal salvation of your children should be a major priority of your life.

We as husbands must realize that our greatest rewards or our greatest rebukes from God, in the day of judgment, will not only be about how we performed in our careers; but it will be about how we raised the children God has put under our care, and how we treated our wives. Husbands, we are to put more emphasis on our families than we do on our jobs and ministry. We are to make sure we are training our children in the ways of the Lord, and we are living the right type of lifestyle before them. God considers our children as clean and holy, and we as fathers must be careful of how we treat that which God considers clean and holy.

2. The husband is to please his wife.

*33. But he that is married careth for the things that are of the world, **how he may please his wife.** (1ˢᵗ Corinthians.7:33)*

Men, when you enter into marriage, you need to realize you are entering into a holy covenant agreement where you will be required by God to try to please your wife. We usually marry someone who we think will bring us happiness for life; God wants us to take the attitude that we are marrying someone who we will try to please for the rest of her life. We are to do all we can to please our wives, and to make life so wonderful for them that they would really enjoy being married unto us.

To please your wife, you must seek God in prayer, asking Him to reveal unto you the necessary things to do. You should often ask your wife what things you can do to bring her pleasure and happiness. Try to get to know your wife so well that you will automatically know what to do, and when to do it, to make her happy. Make pleasing her a priority in your life, and every day, seek to do something special that you know will please her.

It will take energy, effort, time, imagination, and hard work to constantly please your wife. Oftentimes, you will have to go out of your way to do things for her, and you may be required to do things you don't really enjoy doing (like shopping). Also, you may have to make some changes within yourself that you had not planned on making. If there is something about you that displeases your wife, you should be willing to change it. We often take the attitude that "if she does not love me the way I am; it is just too bad for her." That should never be the attitude you take.

Change in you the things she does not like, and seek to grow and develop into the type of person she will be well pleased with. You and she should discuss these things, and she should allow you to do certain things that she may not be happy about but can live with. Make sure, however, those things are not sinful. It will not always be easy to change your habits and actions, but in order to please your wife, there are certain changes that you will have to make within yourself.

As a husband, you must realize God is seeking to make your wife happy, and He gave you to her as part of what He is doing to bring her happiness. You are sent by God to her so He can work through you to make her happy and content. While you are not the total source of her happiness, you are a part of what God is using to bring her happiness. Remember, you represent Jesus Christ in this marriage. Jesus is always doing things to please His bride, the church; and therefore, you too are to always do things that will please your bride.

Husbands, you are never to do anything sinful when seeking to please your wife. God sent you to her with the intention that you remain holy and clean. You are to always do right, and to seek to get her to always do what is right in the eyes of God. Sinful things sometimes bring pleasure for a moment, but the end result is death and destruction, and it displeases God. Never displease God when trying to please your wife.

You must work to please your wife even when she is doing nothing to try to please you. You don't please her because she is pleasing you; you seek to please her because it is something God wants you to do. There may be times when you will think she is not worthy of your efforts to try to please her; however, when these times come, remember you are not worthy of God trying to please you, but He does it anyway. Trying to please your wife is not a reward she earns; it is an instruction from God a husband is required to fulfill.

Once you as a husband have done all you know to please your wife and she is still not pleased or satisfied, realize it is not your fault, and you must place her into the hands of God. You are only part of what God is using to try to bring joy and contentment into her life. Make sure you have done all you can, and be satisfied in knowing you have done your best. Never give up trying, and never give up hope. Continue to hope, continue to pray, and continue to love her. One of the deepest hurts and greatest pains a husband can feel is the pain of trying to satisfy and please his wife, and then discovering she is still not happy. Oftentimes, he becomes confused, and he does not know what to do. He doesn't know where to go to get help or how to ease his pain.

Husbands, it is impossible to satisfy a woman who just refuses to be satisfied. If she cannot find satisfaction within her God and within herself, she will never find satisfaction in you. You are not greater than God. If God cannot make her happy with who He is, with the things He has done for her, and with the things He has given her, neither can you make her happy with who you are, with the things you have done for her, and with the things you have given her. God will not break nor change her free will. If it is not her will to be happy in her God or in herself, God is not going to force her to be happy in you.

For her to be happy and content, it must start within herself. She has to first realize the goodness of God in her life. You need to constantly tell her of how good her God is and of how good he has been to her. Seek to get her to appreciate and to enjoy God. Next, seek to get her to appreciate and enjoy herself. Tell her how beautiful she is to you. Reassure her that she is a person of great worth and value. Always tell her of her good qualities and that you believe she is the best woman on earth for you. Sometimes, she may feel that other women are better than she is, and she may be suffering from low self-esteem. Let her know that there is not a woman on earth better than her. Let her know that she, to you, is better than all women on earth.

Knowing your wife is not satisfied and happy with you can cause great pain within your heart. It can cause you to feel less than a man, and it can make you wonder if there is something wrong with you. You feel helpless and want to give up. It robs you of your joy and tries to draw you down into depression. It tempts you to become unsatisfied with her and to give up on the marriage.

To overcome these negative feelings and emotions, you must (1) see trying to please her as a challenge to be enjoyed; (2) find some things you can do to her and for her that both of you will enjoy doing; (3) learn to be happy with who you are because you are becoming more and more like Christ; and (4) realize that even though Christ is perfect and is the best person in existence (He is God), there are some saints who are not happy and satisfied with Him. If some in the church are not happy and satisfied with Him, it is not a strange thing that some wives are not happy and satisfied with their husbands when their husbands are trying to be like Christ.

3. My personal quest of trying to please my wife

One of the most challenging but greatest joys in my life is trying to please my wife. When I learned that it is God's desire for husbands to please their wives, I made it a major priority of mine to seek to please her. I looked at it as a challenge to be enjoyed and an adventure to be cherished. It became fun trying to think of things to do and then making plans to get those things done. It became an adventure going to different restaurants for an evening dinner or for a quick lunch. Giving special gifts to her for no special reason brought a great delight to my heart. Trying to be romantic again was really a thrill. Taking walks together, holding her while we watch television, and conversing with her quietly, brought new joy and fulfillment within my heart. Although I did these things (and more) for her, I could still tell that at times she was still not happy or satisfied. She was content, but she still was not totally happy.

Instead of being discouraged, I did not give up; I kept doing special things for her, and I begin to work on improving myself. I stopped doing all the things that I knew displeased God and her. Cursing, drinking, staying out late, and working too hard and too long were things that I put out of my life. Neglecting the children and the wife were now things of the past. I also sought to make myself godlier and more intelligent. After looking at the changes I made to please her, I found that I pleased myself also. I am happier with the new person that I am now than I ever was with the person I used to be. In seeking to improve myself to please her, I also embarked on new challenges in life that have brought me great joy and satisfaction.

One such challenge was the challenge of trying to beautify my home. Putting up wallpaper, installing floor tile, and doing other projects around the house were challenges that brought my wife and me great satisfaction. Doing yard work and building things to beautify the home and property became rewarding and fun adventures that she and I both enjoyed.

Another thing that I did in seeking to improve myself was to start reading books on the duties and functions of a husband and a father. Until I started doing this, I never knew reading could be so much fun and so rewarding. I became a better husband, father, and person. Even my boss and coworkers noticed the difference. Also, I ventured into the area of book writing. There were many other things I sought to accomplish because I wanted to become a man my wife could be proud of and happy with. God used my seeking to obey Him, by trying to please my wife, to make a better and happier person out of me.

There are some husbands who have tried everything they could to make their wives happy and satisfied, but their wives are still unhappy. Every husband is not to do the things I have done, but they are to seek God for themselves, asking Him what they should do. Different marriages require different things, and you must find out what things your marriage requires. After doing all you know to do and she still is not happy and satisfied, maybe the problem is not you, but something that may have happened in her past.

Many women have been hurt and have had bad experiences with men while they were young. Their fathers may have mistreated them, abused them, or abandoned them. They found many faults in their father, or in other men involved in their past life. These women then grew up, married, and unknowingly carried those hurts and bad experiences into their marriages. They felt their husbands should be the perfect man, and he should never make the same mistakes as their fathers had, or as the other men that were in their lives had. After being married a short while, they realize that their husbands are not perfect men. Sometimes, their husbands make the same mistakes as other men, and they oftentimes make more mistakes than other men do.

Once she realizes that her husband is no better than the others, she develops a negative attitude towards him, and refuses to be satisfied by him. She feels that if she gives him her heart, he will just hurt it as others did. Husbands, love her with all of your heart, and do the best you can for her. Let her know you are not perfect, but you still love her, even with all of your imperfections. Constantly pray that God will deliver her from the hurts of the past, and from the false expectations of perfection that she has for her present husband.

4. The husband is to remember that he and his wife are bound together for life.

[39] *The wife is bound by the law as long as her husband liveth; but if her husband be dead, she is at liberty to be married to whom she will; only in the Lord. (1st Corinthians. 7:39)*

Marriage is a bond that is to last a lifetime. The strength of that bond, which is supposed to hold the marriage together, is the set of laws and commands God gives concerning marriage. Love is to be only one facet of the strength of that bond, because time and circumstances can cause love to diminish. Even when the love has diminished, a couple should strive to stay together (and rekindle their love) because it is a command of God. If you can't stay together for love, you should be able to stay together because God told you to.

Everything that happens in a marriage should be based on the commands and laws of God. We stay together because God tells us to stay together. We love each other because God tells husbands to love their wives and for wives to learn to love their husbands. We treat each other right because God commanded us to. We submit to each other because God tells us to. If you want a successful marriage, strive to live up to obeying the commands and laws of God. A successful marriage is one in which you are doing what God tells you to do. A successful and lasting marriage is one that is held together by keeping and obeying the commands and laws of God.

Father; a praying man is a powerful man. Please transform me into a powerful man of prayer who prays effectual, fervent, and faith-filled prayers to Your glory in Jesus' name by the power of the Holy Spirit. In Jesus' name I pray; amen.

Jesus my LORD; my marriage has been saved and made better, because I persisted in prayer to the Father in Your name. Prayer changed me, changed my wife, and changed my marriage for the better. Thank You for giving us Your name in prayer.

^{13}And whatsoever ye shall ask in my name, that will I do, that the Father may be glorified in the Son. ^{14}If ye shall ask any thing in my name, I will do it. (John.14:13-14).

Jesus is LORD

CHAPTER 6

Leading and Loving Your Wife like Christ Does the Church

1. The husband is to be the head of his wife like Christ is the head of the church.

2. The husband is to love his wife like Christ loves the church.
   A. The Christ-like love is a love one does not have to earn nor deserve.
   B. The Christ-like love is a love that loves even when it does not receive love in return
   C. The Christ-like love is a love that shows.
   D. The Christ-like love is a love that is constantly at its highest point.
   E. The Christ-like love is a love that never ends.
   F. The Christ-like love is a love based on emotions and feelings, but greatest of all, it is based on commitment.
   G. The Christ-like love is based on the Father in heaven.
   H. The Christ-like love is a love that is faithful to one bride.
   I. The Christ-like love is a love that is the greatest love you will ever experience

God's Divine Instructions To Husbands and Men

1. The husband is to be the head of his wife like Christ is the head of the church.

*²³ For **the husband is the head of the wife, even as Christ is the head of the church:** and he is the saviour of the body. (Ephesians.5:23)*

In the New Testament book of Ephesians, chapter five, the comparison is constantly made between the role of the husband and his wife, and the role of Christ and His bride, the church (The church is the bride of Christ). The underlining message is that a Christian marriage is to be a reflection of the relationship Jesus Christ has with His church. The husband is to represent Christ while the wife is to represent the church. No husband can be called a good or successful husband until he begins to treat his wife as Jesus treats His bride, the church.

When a sinner looks at the way a Christian husband treats his wife and asks him, "Why do you treat her so good?" the Christian husband should be able to say, "I treat my wife so good because I'm trying to treat her as Jesus treats His bride the church." He should also tell the sinner, "If you become a Christian, Jesus will treat you just as good as and even better than I treat my wife. Jesus will love you just as much and even more than I love my wife. Jesus will protect you, provide for you, and make a better person out of you just as I seek to do for my wife." Christian husbands, the standard you need to achieve regarding the way you treat your wife is the standard Jesus sets in the way He treats His bride, the church.

You as a Christian husband have a higher standard than the world. You are to treat your wife better than, show her more love than, and cherish her more than any sinner does his wife. While this may be a standard that seems impossible to reach, it really is one you can achieve because the Holy Ghost is within you to help you accomplish it. The one major question you should ask yourself is, "Am I willing to try with God's help?"

God commands the husband to be the head of his wife just as Christ is the head of His bride, the church. To be the head means to be the highest authority over (with only Christ and God the Father higher). To be the head means to rule over, to lead, and to be in charge of. While many people feel that the wife and husband should be equal and that one should not rule over the other, the headship position of the man over the wife is a God-ordained position that Christians should adhere to.

Husbands, the headship position is not a position you demand to get, nor is it one you must take. It is a position you already possess. Jesus never demands that we give Him the headship position nor does He take it by force. It is a position that is already His, and He just walks in that position. You are not trying to become the head of your wife; you are already her head. You just need to learn what being the head is, and how to fulfill and execute the duties that comes with that position.

As the head of the church, Jesus lets us know what He requires of us and then lets us decide if we will meet His requirements or not. He tells us of the blessings that will happen to us if we do as He says and warns us of the trouble to come if we disobey. He then loves us so much and shows His love to us in such ways that it encourages us to want to obey Him. Husbands, if you show your wife enough love and only require things that are best for her, she may, in return, submit to your headship. However, if she doesn't submit to your headship, leave it up to God to deal with her; and do not try to force her to submit.

When you as a husband walk in the headship position, you do not walk alone; God walks with you. If you are seeking to do your job as the head of the family and your wife rebels, you can rest assured God will get involved and deal with her. Do not try to deal with her in an adverse way nor try to force her to submit to your God-ordained headship position. You do your job as commanded by God (through His written Word), and then leave the rest up to God.

One of the ways Jesus gets us to obey Him is to teach us His Word and His ways. The more we learn of God, the more we obey Him. There should be certain times when you sit with your wife and teach her spiritual principles and precepts from the Word of God. In teaching her the Word of God, you should also show her in the Bible why you do the things you do, and why she should respect your position and submit to it. Let her know to rebel against it is to rebel against God. Seek to help her understand that her major reason for submitting is because God tells her to. Also, show her that the things you ask of her are only for the best. Never ask her to do something in violation of the Word or the ways of God. Jesus tells us that if we love Him, we will keep his commandments.

[15] ***If ye love me, keep my commandments.*** [21] ***He that hath my commandments, and keepeth them, he it is that loveth me:*** *and he that loveth me shall be loved of my Father, and I will love him, and will manifest myself to him. (John 14:15, 21)*

Jesus bases our obedience to Him through our love for Him, and our love for His Father. He lets us know that He and the Father will love us when we obey Him. Jesus makes it a love thing. Reveal to your wife that her submission to you shows her love for you and her love for God. Let her know also that because she submits to your headship position, God really loves her for it, and you do too. Husbands, to get your wife to submit to you, make it a love thing; and never make it a demanding and forcing thing.

Also, remember while seeking to get your wife to submit to you, one of the wisest things you can do is to always value and respect her opinion. While you are the head and are responsible for leading the family, you are not to belittle or ignore the suggestions and opinions of your wife. To be the head does not mean you have to know everything, nor does it mean you have to make all of the decisions. Seek your wife's opinions, and ask her for suggestions when making a decision for the family. It is much easier for a wife to submit to her husband when she knows that he includes her when making decisions and when leading the family.

Another way Jesus Christ gets us to submit to His headship and to obey Him is by being the type of person we would want to submit to and obey. Husbands, when trying to get your wife to submit to you, not only make it a love thing, but also seek to become the type of person she would want to submit to and obey. That is why Jesus tells you to treat her like He treats the church. The more we act like Jesus, and the more we become what Jesus is, the more our wives may want to submit to and obey our headship position. Daily study the written Word of God to learn character qualities which will cause your wife to want to submit to you. Learn what you must do to become more like Jesus.

If we as husbands are going to walk in the headship position which God ordained for us to walk in, we must teach our wives the Word of God, make headship and submission a love thing, and be the type of person they would want to submit to.

In order for a man to claim his position as head of his wife, he must be the type of head that Christ is to His bride, the church. If he is not treating her as Christ is treating His church, he cannot claim the headship position. Husbands, your God-ordained headship position is not given just because you are a husband; it is given because you are a husband who treats his wife as Christ treats His church. If you are not treating her as Christ treats His church, you are not to claim the headship position, and don't expect her to submit to you.

2. The husband is to love his wife like Christ loves the church.

²⁵ *Husbands, love your wives,* **even as Christ also loved the church,** *and gave himself for it. (Ephesians. 5:25)*

Once again, the comparison to Christ and the church is made. God is reinforcing the fact that a husband is to deal with his wife like Christ deals with the church. Christ sets the standards for us to reach as husbands. Husbands, if you want a good and successful marriage, your main objectives should be (1) to learn all you can about the personality of Christ, (2) to learn how He deals with His church, and (3) to seek to be like Jesus and to do as Jesus does. **_Jesus is the key to what a husband is to be._**

God tells husbands they are to love their wives like Christ loves His church. To love means to have a deep emotional attraction for. It also means doing what is good and best for your wife. Many men will stress the fact that they are to be the head, and they will stress the fact that the wife is to submit, but they never stress the fact that they are to love her like Christ loves the church. They can teach a woman how to submit, but they cannot teach themselves how to love their wives like Christ loves the church. Husbands, you should know more about how to love your wife like Christ loves the church, than you do about how a wife is to submit to her husband.

Because God tells husbands to love their wives like Christ loves the church, husbands must learn about the kind of love Jesus shows the church, and then to be sure to love his wife that way. Husbands, you cannot obey if you do not know what to do or how to do it. Also, husbands, you must realize that if God tells you to do something and you don't do it, you are committing sin. In order to help keep you from sinning, we will endeavor to teach you the attributes of the Christ-like love, but it is up to you to apply it into your marriage and life. While there are many attributes of the Christ-like love, we will only discuss a few of the outstanding ones. These are not all that He possesses, but these are enough to get husbands started on the right track.

A. The Christ-like love is a love one does not have to earn nor deserve.

Even when we were sinners and doing things that displeased Jesus, He still loved us. We did not deserve His love, we were not trying to earn His love, and we were everything Jesus did not want us to be. We were not trying to please Him, we were not seeking Him, and we really did not want Him. Regardless of all that, Jesus still loved us with the greatest love He had. Your wife may not be everything you want her to be, and there may be things about her you do not like. You may also feel she has gotten to the point where she is not worthy of you nor of your love. Even if, in your opinion, your wife may not deserve your love and may be many of the things you wish she wasn't, you are to love her with your greatest love. She does not have to try to earn your love nor is she to try to deserve your love. You are to love her because God tells you to have that Christ-like love, which is a love one does not have to earn nor deserve.

In order to love your wife when she has not earned nor deserved it, you must do as Christ does:

1) Focus on her good points.
2) Give grace concerning her bad points.
3) Use the Word of God to teach her and yourself how to become better people.

Also, realize you are not as good as you think you are, and maybe in her eyes, you are not worthy of her love either. She too should be focusing on your good points, giving you grace for your bad points, and should be teaching you from the Word of God how you and she can become better people. Christ loves you, and you didn't earn it nor deserve it. Your wife loves you, and you did not earn it nor deserve it. Therefore, you must love your wife even when she doesn't earn it nor deserves it.

B. The Christ-like love is a love that loves even when it does not receive love in return

Jesus loved us even when we did not deserve it, earn it, nor return it. We live in a society where a husband's love for his wife is based on her love for him. If she stops loving her husband, her husband will stop loving her. If he starts loving her and she does not return his love, he usually stops loving her. God so loved the world that He gave His only begotten son Jesus Christ. Not everyone in the world loves God, but He loves them and always does good things to them even when they do not return love unto Him.

As a husband seeking to develop the Christ-like love, you must love your wife even when she refuses to love you back. Men are creatures that make mistakes and do things that sometimes cause their wife's love for them to diminish. There will be times when your wife will not love you as she should. When you realize she no longer loves you, you will be tempted to stop loving her and to walk out. Husbands, you are to love your wife even when she does not return love to you.

The reason you love Christ now is because even when you refused to return His love, He kept loving you, seeking after you, and seeking after your love. If Jesus had given up loving you because you would not return His love, you would be doomed to an eternal lake of fire. If you love your wife and keep seeking after her and her love (as Christ kept loving you and kept seeking after you and your love), she may eventually start loving you like you started loving Christ. If you stop loving her because she will not return your love, your marriage may be doomed to a sad end.

C. The Christ-like love is a love that shows.

Jesus constantly does things to show us that He loves us. He doesn't just say He loves us; He does things to show it. One of the things Jesus did to show us His love was to die for us and rise again. Jesus did the greatest thing that could ever be done to show His love for us. Have you done the greatest thing you can do to show your wife you love her? What great sacrifices have you made for her lately? What great, wonderful, and needed things are you doing for her that will cause her to know, without any reasonable doubt, that you love her? You should live your life in such ways that she will never be able to question your love for her or your loyalty to her.

One of the ways to determine what great and needed sacrifices to make for your wife (which will show how much you love her) is to notice her greatest needs and then fulfill those needs. Jesus noticed that the greatest need of mankind was to be delivered from sin, from the devil, and from eternal damnation, and then to be saved and reconciled back to God forever. After seeing that need, Jesus did all He could do to fulfill that need. Once we noticed that it was Jesus who fulfilled our greatest need, we came to love Him for it. Once your wife sees that you are seeking to fulfill her greatest needs, she may in return love you for it.

Jesus constantly and daily shows His love for us. Are you constantly and daily showing your love for your wife? Many husbands have "lip service of love" but no "actions of love." Every day, Jesus shows us actions of love because actions speak louder than words. Every day, you should be doing things for your wife that will show her you love her. Do big things, do little things, do different things; but make sure that every day, you do something geared at showing her you love her. If you are going to have the Christ-like love, it must be a love that does the greatest things it can; and it must be a love that is seen constantly, daily, and openly.

Did you stop at any time today to notice the many things that Jesus has done for you today to show you He loves you? Did you stop long enough to say thank You Lord? If you become upset when you do something special to show your wife you love her, but she doesn't notice it, how do you think Jesus feels when you do not notice the many things He has done for you today, to show you He loves you?

D. The Christ-like love is a love that is constantly at its highest point.

From the time Jesus started loving us to this very moment, His love for us has always been at its maximum point. He loves us as much today as He ever did. You as a husband must love your wife as much as you can, all the time. Your love is to never decrease, and the only reason it increases is because you have learned how to love her more today than you knew yesterday. You are never to love her less today than you did at any time in the past. You can only love her more in the future because you may, in the future, learn how to love her more.

Maximum love is a Christ-like love that a husband needs to learn to develop. Love is not just something you fall into; it is something you can learn to do. God tells the older women to teach the younger women how to learn to love their husbands.

⁴ **_That they may teach the young women_** to be sober, **to love their husbands,** to love their children. (Titus 2:4)

If a woman can be taught to love her husband, a husband can be taught to love his wife to the maximum all the time. Love is also something you choose to do. We as Christians chose to love Jesus while sinners chose not to love Him. Husbands, when you married her, you were also choosing to love her; so learn how to love her to the maximum all the time.

To develop a love that is at its maximum point all of the time, you must begin with a deep-rooted determination that comes from your heart. You must make up in your mind that you are going to love your wife to the fullest at all times. Next, you must daily tell her you love her because constantly saying it will reinforce it within your own heart and mind. Maximum love is based more on you than it is on the person you love. Christ's maximum love is based on His own decision to love us; not on us being so good that it causes Him to love us. Maximum love comes from within, and is not based on things from without.

E. The Christ-like love is a love that never ends.

Jesus Christ will never stop loving you, so you are never to stop loving your wife. You must work at maintaining your love for her, and you must work on never allowing your love for her to end. To do that, you must not depend on her doing things that will cause you to keep loving her; you must do things yourself that will cause you to keep on loving her, regardless of what may happen. Once again, you must constantly tell her you love her, and you must constantly do things to show you love her. Also, let her know your love for her will always remain, always grow, and will never end.

A husband's love for his wife does not end in one day. It usually takes a period of time for a husband to stop loving his wife. Also, there are signs that tell him his love for her is diminishing. Things she does begin to annoy him more and more. He spends much time away from her, and he stops doing nice and romantic things for her. He also stops telling her he loves her, and he ceases doing things that a person in love normally does. If these and other signs start showing up in your life, you must recognize them and overcome them.

Realize that if you continue on that path, you will end up not loving your wife, and you will end up not fulfilling God's divine instructions to husbands concerning loving their wives like Christ loves the church. Many people think love is an emotion that cannot be controlled. They feel a person can helplessly fall in love and can also helplessly fall out of love. Love is a choice and not just an uncontrollable emotion. Love is something you can choose to do as well as choose to maintain.

4. **_That they may teach the young women_** to be sober, **_to love their husbands,_** to love their children. *(Titus 2:4)*

You chose to love her and not to love someone else. You chose to love Jesus and God and not to love some other god. Others choose not to love your wife, your Jesus, and your God. Love is a choice that you have the power to make, so choose to love your wife, and choose never to stop loving her.

F. The Christ-like love is a love based on emotions and feelings, but greatest of all, it is based on commitment.

Christ is a savior that makes commitments and keeps His commitments. He is committed to obeying His Father, and because of that commitment, He always obeys him. Christ is committed to loving us, and because of that commitment, He always loves us. Regardless of what may happen, Christ will always obey His Father. Regardless of what may happen or what we may do, Christ will always love us. The reason He always obeys His Father and always loves us is because, He doesn't base His actions on emotions and feelings only; He bases them on the fact that He made a commitment, and that He will fulfill that commitment.

There may be times when your feelings and emotions for your wife may decrease, change for the worse, or even vanish completely; but if you are committed to loving her, you will never leave her. If you are committed to loving her, you will also be determined to do what it takes to cause your feelings and emotions to return. You will also do what it takes to cause your feelings and emotions of love for her to remain strong, and to increase. Do not base your love on feelings and emotions only; but also base it on commitment.

How committed are you to maintaining your feelings of love for your wife? How committed are you to increase in your feelings of love for your wife? Always remember that the greatest part of love is commitment.

G. The Christ-like love is based on the Father in heaven.

Although Jesus loves us, He also loves His Father. All of the things Jesus did were based on His love for His Father. Because he loved His Father, Jesus would face the agony of the Cross (even when He would have preferred another way). Jesus would do something for His Father when He would not do it for Himself. Your love for your wife should be based on your love for your Heavenly Father. When your love is based on the Father, you will do things for Him that you wouldn't do for yourself. You would even love your wife with all of your heart because your Heavenly Father told you to (even when at times, you really don't want to love her at all). A Christ-like love is a love based more on the Father than it is on anything or anyone else.

Do you love your heavenly Father enough to obey Him in everything? Even obey Him concerning the way you treat your wife?

H. The Christ-like love is a love that is faithful to one bride.

Jesus has only one bride, which is the church. He is faithful to that one bride and will not love another. Husbands, you are to forsake all others and love your own wife and her only. You are to love no other woman as much as or in the same way you love your wife. You are to guard against developing a relationship that could eventually grow into an affair. Turn down all advancements that other women may make toward you, and live your life in such ways that all females will know that you have no intentions of ever cheating on your wife. As a husband, you are commanded by God to love your wife like Christ loves the church, and the Christ-like love is a love that loves his own wife and her only.

Husbands, to love your wife as Christ loves the church is not an option for you; it is an instruction of God that you need to obey. Regardless of the circumstances and regardless of how she is treating you, you are to love her like Christ loves the church. Never base your love for her on her love for you. If Jesus based His love for us on our love for Him, He would not love us with as great a love as He does. If Jesus loves us only when we do right, He would not love us with as great a love as He does.

The love that Jesus has is based on His choosing to love us with all of His heart, regardless of how we are and regardless of what we do. Husbands, if you have not been loving your wife like Christ loves the church, (1) you have committed sin, (2) you need to repent, (3) you need to ask for forgiveness, and (4) you need to begin loving your wife like Christ loves the church. God will forgive you, and He will help you to begin loving your wife in the same manner as Christ loves His bride, the church. Have you determined that by the power of the Holy Ghost, you will strive to love your wife like Christ loves the church?

I. The Christ-like love is a love that is the greatest love you will ever experience

The greatest love you will ever experience is the love of Jesus Christ, because it is the love of God flowing through Him. There is no greater love than the Father, and there is no greater love than Jesus Christ. Because husbands are commanded to love their wives as Christ loves the church; a husband's love should be the greatest love his wife will ever experience (other than the love of God).

While it seems impossible, a husband's love should be equal to, or greater than even a mother's love. Husbands are not commanded to love their wives as a mother loves her child, husbands are commanded to love their wives as Christ loves the church. Because Christ's love is greater than a mother's love, a husband's love for his wife should be greater than a mother's love. Wives should be able to say of their husbands, "This man loves me as much as my mother does, and he is truly trying to love me like Christ loves the church".

Only by the power of the Holy Spirit can one keep this commandment. Therefore; all Christian husbands must pray asking God to keep them filled with the Holy Spirit; and to empower them by the Holy Spirit to love their wives as Christ loves the church.

¹³ I can do all things through Christ which strengtheneth me. (Philippians.4:13).

Husbands, can you truly say that the greatest earthly love your wife has ever experienced is your love? Can your wife tell that you are trying to love her like Christ loves the church? Can your wife tell that you, by the power of the Holy Spirit, are trying to give her the greatest earthly love that she will ever experience?

Father; if it is not about love; it is not about You. I want my marriage to be all about You, therefore; it must be all about love. I want "me" to be all about You; therefore, I must be all about love. Thank You for teaching me many of the attributes of the Christ-like love. By the power of the Holy Ghost, I purpose to implement these teachings into my heart and life. In Jesus' name I pray; amen.

⁷Beloved, let us love one another: for love is of God; and every one that loveth is born of God, and knoweth God. ⁸He that loveth not knoweth not God; for God is love. (1ˢᵗ John.4:7-8)

Jesus my LORD; to walk in love is to walk in You. I must always walk in You (in love) so all will know I am truly one of Your disciples.

³⁴A new commandment I give unto you, That ye love one another; as I have loved you, that ye also love one another. ³⁵By this shall all men know that ye are my disciples, if ye have love one to another. (John.13:34-35).

Jesus is LORD

CHAPTER 7

Giving Yourself Totally to Your Wife

1. The husband is to give himself for his wife.

2. A husband discovering his faults and improving himself.

3. Using the Word and circumstances to improve your spouse.

4. When seeking to improve your wife, never hit her; never abuse her physically, verbally, mentally or emotionally; and never do anything that will bring her pain or hurt.

5. Goals to try to achieve when seeking to improve your spouse.

6. Sanctifying your wife.

7. Helping your wife to rise above her faults and sins so her lifestyle will be clean in the sight of God and men.

8. Appearance and personality

9. The husband is to seek to make his wife a better person.

God's Divine Instructions To Husbands and Men

1. The husband is to give himself for his wife.

25 Husbands, love your wives, even as Christ also loved the church, and gave himself for it. (Ephesians.5:25)

While it is possible to give without loving, it is impossible to love without giving. When you give from a heart of love, you give the greatest things that you can. Jesus loved so much that He gave His greatest sacrifice when He died and rose for the church. It was a sacrifice motivated by love. Husbands, you need to be like Jesus and give the greatest sacrifices you can to your wife. Regardless of the cost and regardless of the pain, you as a husband should be willing to give your wife the greatest things you can. Jesus gave greatly, and I love Him greatly for it. If you give greatly to your wife, she may love you greatly for it.

When we think of Jesus giving Himself for His church, we only think of His crucifixion. We often fail to realize all of the other ways Jesus gives of Himself for His church, and how He does it every day. Giving yourself for your wife is not a one-time sacrifice; it is a constant sacrifice that you as a husband must continually give. Jesus continually gives us His blessings and protection. He is continually doing things for us, with us, to us, in us, and through us. There is never a time or moment that Jesus is not giving Himself for His bride the church. To give yourself to your wife will require that you make great sacrifices for her, and that you make continual sacrifices for her.

All that Jesus Christ does is for two purposes: (1) to please and obey His Father because He loves Him; and (2) to protect, perfect, prepare, and provide for His bride, the church, because He loves her. Everything you do as a husband should be for three major purposes: (1) for your God, (2) for your wife, and (3) for your children. When you go to work, it should be for those three purposes: to please God, wife, and children. Even the things that you do for yourself should be things that will help to make you a better person for your God, wife, and children. When you do things to help others who are in need or whenever you show Christian love, it should glorify God and please your wife (she should be pleased to see that she has a husband who shows Christian love toward others). When you became a Christian, your life no longer belonged to you. It belonged to God.

19 *What? know ye not that your body is the temple of the Holy Ghost which is in you, which ye have of God, and ye are not your own? 20 For ye are bought with a price: therefore glorify God in your body, and in your spirit, which are God's. (1ˢᵗ Corinthians.6:19-20)*

When you became a Christian husband, your life no longer belonged to you; it belonged to God and to your wife, and everything you do is to be done for the glory of your God and for your wife and family. While you as a husband are busy giving things to your wife, don't forget to give her yourself. The greatest gift you can ever give to your wife is yourself. To give her possessions and money but not give her yourself is to give her less than the very best. She did not marry possessions and money. She married you. When you gave her nothing but yourself, she loved you so much she wanted to marry you. Now that she is married to you, don't make the mistake of thinking she is no longer satisfied with you, but it is things that now satisfies her. Things may make her feel happy, but it is only you that can make her feel loved.

2. The husband is to seek to make his wife a better person.

That he might sanctify and cleanse it with the washing of water by the word, That he might present it to himself a glorious church, not having spot, or wrinkle, or any such thing; but that it should be holy and without blemish. (Ephesians.5:26-27)

It is God's desire that your wife becomes a better person because she is married to you, therefore your goal should be to try to develop your wife into a better and godlier person. However, before you can effectively make your wife a better person, you must first work to become a better person yourself. Jesus tells us to first remove the beam out of our eye before we try to remove the mote out of someone else's eye. We as men are quick to criticize our wives for their faults, yet we fail to see our own faults. We think we are perfect, and they are not. There should be times when we seek to discover what our faults are, and then work to correct them.

3. A husband discovering his faults and improving himself

In order to find out what your faults are and how to correct them, you must begin with prayer and the Word of God. You must pray and ask God to reveal your faults to you and to show you how to correct them. When you ask God to reveal your faults, do not expect Him to reveal all of them at one time. He may show them to you little by little. As you work to correct the ones revealed to you, He will begin to show you more. Don't become discouraged at your many faults; just thank God He is working in you and with you to correct them all.

Also, when seeking to correct and improve yourself, read the Word of God on a daily basis to learn what God desires of you. As you learn what His desires are for you and your life, you should get busy working to fulfill them. Another thing you may need to do is to ask those who know you the best. Always begin by asking your wife. Then ask others who are godly and know you very well. When they reveal your faults unto you, do not get angry and do not rebel. Take note of what they say, realize they may be right, and then make the needed changes.

Oftentimes, it is very hard for you to listen to your wife. You notice her faults and think she is not qualified to mention yours. You must realize that your wife loves you, and she only wants the best for you. She is also the closest person to you and she knows you the best. She sees and knows things about you that others don't know, and she sees and knows things that you may not admit to yourself.

Ask her of your faults, and then respect her opinions as she relates them to you. When your wife, your God, and others reveal to you your faults, don't hide behind excuses or reasons why you are as you are; just seek to accept what they say and then correct the faults. To give excuses and reasons will only cause you to remain the same, but to make changes will cause you to grow and become better.

You do not have to wait until you reach perfection before you start trying to help your wife become a better person; you just need to be sure you are trying to become a better person yourself, and that your wife sees that you are trying to improve. Do not ask her to try to improve herself if you are not trying to improve yourself as well. Once your wife sees you are trying to improve, she may help you, and she may also seek to improve herself. When she sees you making the changes she says you need to make, she may begin making the changes you say she needs to make.

4. Using the Word and circumstances to improve your spouse

When seeking to improve your wife, the main tool you are to use is the Word of God. You can also use other resources such as books, sermons, and seminars; but all are to be based on the Word of God and its correct interpretation. These tools are to be used with love, patience, tenderness, and grace. Jesus uses His Word to improve you; and He does it with love, patience, tenderness and grace. Thus, when you use these things to improve your wife, you are being like Christ.

Also, remember to use the circumstances you and your wife goes through as an opportunity to help her improve. When using circumstances to improve your spouse, you should always relate those circumstances to the Word of God. Show her how God allowed (or caused) what happened to her to happen, so He can speak to her, and help her to become all He wants her to be. Be there to help her, comfort her, and support her in all that she does. Let her know you are never against her, and that whatever happens in her life, God, she, and you will make it through together.

5. When seeking to improve your wife, never hit her; never abuse her physically, verbally, mentally or emotionally; and never do anything that will bring her pain or hurt

When seeking to improve your wife, never hit her; never abuse her physically, verbally, mentally or emotionally; and never do anything that will bring her pain or hurt. While you are her husband, you are not her God, and she is not a little child for you to spank. No abuse of any kind is to ever be done by you. If she refuses to improve for the better, pray and leave her in the hands of God. God will deal with her in His timing and in His own way.

6. Goals to try to achieve when seeking to improve your spouse

In your attempt to improve your wife, there are certain goals you want to accomplish. These goals are the same goals Jesus has for His church. These goals are (1) to sanctify her to God and to you, (2) to cleanse her from sins, (3) to present her to yourself and to God as a glorious person, (4) to cause her to live holy, and (5) to help cause her to be without blemish. These are not all the goals a husband should strive to accomplish for his wife, but they are the ones given in this passage and are the ones that will be instrumental in helping her to become all God wants her to become.

7. Sanctifying your wife

A wife should be sanctified to her God, to her husband, and to her children. There are other things she may be sanctified to, but these are the three major ones. The word sanctified means "to set apart for a specific purpose". Husbands, you should always try to sanctify your wife and yourself to God. This begins with her salvation and yours. Your major goal is to do all you can to be sure she and you are Christians. Once she and you become Christians, you both are to help each other grow in your knowledge of Christ, and in your obedience to Christ. You want her to be all God wants her to be, and to do all God wants her to do; while you yourself become all God wants you to be, and seek to do all God wants you to do.

Not only should a wife (and her husband) be sanctified to God, but she also is to be sanctified to her husband, and her husband should be sanctified to her. She is to be totally faithful to him, and he to her; and they both should be working together to make the marriage the best it can be. The best way to accomplish that is by working together to develop a love for God that is so great that you and she will both try to obey Him in everything. The end result of you and her both obeying God is that she will become the type of wife you should want her to be, and you will become the type of husband she should want you to be. This will also cause her to be totally sanctified (set aside) to you, and you sanctified to her.

Husbands and wives should be sanctified to their children if they are parents. Husbands, you are to help your wife to become the best mother she can be, while she works with you to develop you into the best father you can be. You are to help her in every area she asks for help in, and needs help in. Always encourage her and support her. Once again, help her learn from the Word of God what the duties of a mother are and how to perform them. While she is learning the duties of a mother, you must also be learning and performing the duties that the Holy Bible says a father is to perform. When she becomes the type of mother God instructs her to be, and you become the type of father God instructs you to be, you both will become the kind of parent you both should want one another to be.

8. Helping your wife to rise above her faults and sins so her lifestyle will be clean in the sight of God and men.

When you decided to marry your wife, you and she felt that each was perfect with little or no faults or sins; but as you lived with each other, you both discovered that each does have many faults and sins. You and she should notice each other's faults and sins, and then you and she should confess them to God and work together to repent of them. As you help her to repent of all of her faults and sins, and she helps you repent of all of your faults and sins, you both are to remember it will take time, work, and patience. You and she should also work together to help keep each other from developing new faults and sins.

Cleansing of sins comes by the blood of Jesus and by the washing of water by the Word. When a person becomes a Christian, Jesus spiritually washes them in His blood to cleanse them of their sins. After being cleansed in the blood of Jesus, Jesus then uses His Word to constantly cleanse saints of whatever sins that may occur in their everyday lives. He shows them, in His Word, the sinful things they may be doing. When they began to obey the Word and to repent of sin, it was the washing of water by the Word that cleansed them. *Cleansing for salvation is by the blood; cleansing for daily righteous living is by the written Word of God.* Jesus wants a glorious church that is without any spots or wrinkles, or any such things. He wants His bride, the church, to be perfect (the best they can be) and to look good.

9. Appearance and personality

Husbands, not only should you be concerned about the spiritual side of your wife (and of yourself), you should also be concerned about her physical appearance and yours. When a bride comes down the aisle, if there is a big spot on her dress and her dress is wrinkled, it embarrasses her, it embarrasses her husband, and it embarrasses those who love her most. Husbands, always encourage your wife to look her best at all times. Let her know that you and she represents God and each other. Let her know what looks good to you, and what looks holy to God. Allow her to buy some clothes (and other things) that will help enhance her beauty. You should be the main person who helps her to be glorious and glamorous in her physical appearance.

Not only are you both to be glorious in physical appearance, you both are to be glorious in the way that you carry yourselves around people. Your personalities and ways of doing things should bring glory to God and to each other. The word glory means "something that brings praise, value, and honor". Because of the way you and she conduct yourselves, (because of your personalities) when people see you or her, both should bring glory to God because you are Christians and glory to each other because you are married to each other. Husbands, if you want to help your wife bring glory to God and to you, you must get busy doing things that bring glory to God and to her. She may do for you what you do for her. Women are to be followers, and men are to be leaders, so lead your wife into a lifestyle of bringing glory to God and to you. Tell your wife that she is special to God and to you. When you do that, she may begin to act like the special person that she is to God and to you.

One of the greatest attributes a wife can possess is to be holy and to live holy. In order to develop the attribute of holy living, you and she should find a good Bible-teaching church where both can learn and grow together. You must develop a prayer time when the children, she, and you can pray together. As her husband, you should study the Word of God with her. Go over the pastor's sermon with your wife, and find other study materials that will help you and her grow spiritually. With all of that, never forget to be a good Christian example. If you go to church, she may go to church. If you pray, she may pray. If you live holy, she may live holy.

While you as a husband should be seeking to do all you can to help your wife to be holy and live holy, do not feel that it is your fault if she does not live that way. You are not required to make her holy; you are only required to try to do all you can to help her to live holy. The thing you need to ask yourself is, are you doing your best for her? If you are not doing your best, repent of it, and then start doing your best today.

Christ wants His bride to be without blemishes, and you should want your wife to be without blemishes also. A blemish (in this text) means "<u>something sinful within a person that they have the power to remove</u>". There may be things within your wife that are blemishes. If there are such blemishes in her life, you have no choice but to inform her of these things and admonish her to change. Whenever she is involved in things displeasing to God, you must tell her of them. Tell her in love and in grace, and be patient with her as she seeks to change. If she refuses to change, at least you have done your job by telling her and by being a good Christian example.

Although I have said this once, I must say it again: do not expect your wife to be sanctified, clean, glorious, holy, and without blemish for you, if you are not going to be those things for her. Always remember that you, as her husband. are to lead the way, and she is to follow. Jesus was those things first, and then He asked the church to become as He is. He is the leader that the church is to follow. Many husbands are doing all they can to make (or force) their wives to be sanctified, clean, glorious, holy, and without blemish. They are trying many different things; but they are failing to do the one major thing God tells them to do that will help their wives to become sanctified, clean, glorious, holy, and without blemish. The one major thing God tells them to do is to give themselves first to God, and then to their wives. When you give yourself totally and fully to God, and then to your wife, and make her the most special person on earth to you, she may then become a better person for God and for you.

Father; please help me to daily and constantly submit myself to You. Please anoint me by the power of the Holy Ghost to yield every area of my life to You and to Jesus Christ. In Jesus' name I pray; amen.

⁶Humble yourselves therefore under the mighty hand of God, that he may exalt you in due time: (1ˢᵗ Peter.5:6)

Jesus my LORD; thank You for being the kind of Savior that it is easy to submit to. It is easy to submit to love, grace, and mercy. It is easy to submit to blessings, benefits, and privileges. It is easy to submit to the only one who can give us eternal life. I rejoice in daily, constantly, and continually submitting to the Father, to You, and to the Holy Spirit.

Jesus is LORD

Chapter 8

Loving Your Wife as Yourself and Leaving Your Parents

1. The husband is to love his wife as his own body.

2. Loving yourself so that you can love your wife.

3. Treating yourself right so you can treat your wife right.

4. Christ sets the standards husbands are to strive to achieve.

5. A shift in authority.

6. Leaving ungodly influence.

7. Getting a home of your own for you and your wife.

8. A husband is to leave his parents.

God's Divine Instructions To Husbands and Men

1. The husband is to love his wife as his own body.

So ought men to love their wives as their own bodies. *He that loveth his wife loveth himself. For no man ever yet hated his own flesh; but nourisheth and cherisheth it, even as the Lord the church: For we are members of his body, of his flesh, and of his bones.* (Ephesians. 5:28-30)

A great principle of marriage that all need to adhere to is that you are to treat your spouse as good as, or even better than, you treat yourself. You are never to love yourself more than you love your wife, and you are never to do more for yourself than you do for your wife. You are to look at your wife as if she is part of your body, and then treat her as you would treat yourself.

2. Loving yourself so that you can love your wife

In order to love your wife as your own body, you are to first love yourself. Realize you are made as you are, because it's the way God wanted you to be. We often compare ourselves with other people. If we feel we do not look as good as most other people, we think we are ugly. We also compare ourselves with how we think we should look or how we want to look. If we don't look as we think we should look, or if there is something about us we don't like, we say we are unattractive. We need to realize that true beauty is in the eyes of God, and not men. God made you, and He is the one to say what is beautiful and what is not.

God made you in His image, and should you say you are ugly, you are saying God is ugly. When it comes to the physical part of you, realize God is happy with it, and you too should be happy with it. Your job is to make it look as good as you can, and then be happy with it. You can't change what God has done, but you can change what you can do. You can make yourself look the best you can with what God has given you. Not only should you learn to love the way you look outwardly, you should learn to love the way you are inwardly. If you are saved and trying to obey God the best you can, you can rejoice even if you are not all you feel you should be. You can rejoice because God is making you into what He wants you to be.

[20] *Now the God of peace, that brought again from the dead our Lord Jesus, that great shepherd of the sheep, through the blood of the everlasting covenant,* [21] *Make you perfect in every good work to do his will,* **working in you that which is well pleasing in his sight,** *through Jesus Christ; to whom be glory for ever and ever. Amen. (Hebrews. 13:20-21)*

If you can't love how you are now inwardly, you can love the fact that you are on your way to an inward personality that God loves and that you can love too. God wants you to love yourself so you can love your wife as much as you love yourself. When you look at your wife, you are really looking at your own body. She, in the eyes of God, is you; and you are her. To God, she and you are one flesh and one body. Because she and you are one flesh and one body to God, you are to treat her as you would treat yourself, therefore learn to treat yourself the best you can, so you can treat her the best you can.

3. Treating yourself right so you can treat your wife right

The best way to love yourself is to love your wife because when you love your wife, God says you are really loving yourself. Because you should not hate your own body, you should not hate your wife. Because you should not mistreat your own body, you should not mistreat your wife. Because you should not abuse your own body, you should not abuse your wife. Because you should not beat up on yourself, you should not beat up on your wife. You should never curse out yourself; thus, you should never curse out your wife. The things you should not do to yourself are the things you should not do to your wife.

A man nourishes and cherishes his own body, so should he nourish and cherish his wife. We constantly give our bodies the things they need to survive and to stay healthy. Therefore, a husband should give his wife the things she needs that will help her to survive and to stay healthy. We wash our bodies, we put the best clothes on our bodies, we cherish our bodies, and we consider our bodies as precious. That is the way we should treat our wives. We are to cherish our wives, and take as good care of them as we do ourselves.

4. Christ sets the standards husbands are to strive to achieve

Once again, the standard to reach when trying to love your wife as you would love your own body is the standard Jesus sets by loving the church as His own body. If you fall short of treating yourself right, do not use yourself as a standard; use Jesus and the way He treats His bride, the church, as the standard to try to achieve. Maybe you do not treat yourself very well. You may drink alcohol, smoke cigarettes, eat the wrong food, not get enough rest, and abuse your body with sinful lusts. Just because you do not take good care of yourself does not mean you are not to take good care of your wife. You may fall short within yourself, but yourself is not the standard you are trying to meet. Christ is that standard.

When a husband falls short of being what he should be and doing what he should do, God no longer uses him as a standard to try to reach. God then uses His son Jesus Christ as the standard husbands are to try to reach. What God is trying to reveal to husbands is that they are to come up to the level and standards that Christ has set, and then to operate in their marriages on that level and on those standards. Husbands, you are still representing Christ in your marriage, so treat your wife like Christ treats His bride the church, and love her like Christ loves his own body.

5. A husband is to leave his parents.

[31] *For this cause shall a man leave his father and mother. (Ephesians.5:31)*

Every man who is contemplating marriage is instructed by God to leave his parents and be joined to his wife. The proper order of this instruction (or command) of God is for the husband to first leave his parents and then to be joined to his wife. To leave his parents means to do at least three things: (1) leave the authority his parents have over him, (2) leave the ungodly influence his parents have over him, and (3) leave their household and establish a household of his own.

To leave one's parents does not mean to abandon them and to have nothing else to do with them. To leave means that the relationship between him and his parents have changed to one where he loves them, communicates with them, and respects them; but he is no longer under their authority because his greatest loyalty and love (under Christ) is now toward his wife. While there was a strong bond between him and his parents, there is now a stronger bond between him and his wife. The bond that was between him and his parents has been altered.

6. A shift in authority

When a man and a woman unites in marriage, it causes a shift in authority to occur. The authority that is over the woman shifts from her father (or mother if her father is deceased or not a part of the home) to her husband. If she was a single woman who lived in her own home, the authority over her shifts from herself to her husband. The authority that is over the man shifts from his father (or from his mother if his father is deceased or not a part of the home) to himself. If he was not living in his parents' household, then the authority had already shifted to him when he left to start his own home.

The authority we are speaking of here is the authority as granted by God.

1) God is the head (holds authority over) of Christ.
2) Christ is the head of man.
3) Man is the head of the woman.
4) The parents (the father and then the mother) are heads of the children.

[3]But I would have you know, that the head of every man is Christ; and the head of the woman is the man; and the head of Christ is God. (1st Corinthians.11:3)

The father has greater authority over the children than the mother does, and he is held more accountable for their spiritual and physical growth than the mother is. God tells the fathers to provide for the children, and He tells the fathers to raise the children in the nurture and admonition of the Lord. In many homes, it is the mother who is raising the children in the nurture and admonition of the Lord. Husbands, if this is happening in your home, it is time for you to start fulfilling your headship responsibility of spiritually educating your children.

1. When a man gets married, his spiritual authority goes from God over Jesus over his father over his mother over him; to <u>God over Jesus over him</u>.

2. When a woman gets married, her spiritual authority goes from God over Jesus over her father over her mother over her; to <u>God over Jesus over her husband over her</u>.

3. If she leaves her parents home unmarried, the authority is shifted to God over Jesus over her until she gets married.

You as a husband must realize that once you get married, you are no longer under the authority of your parents. They no longer have control over you, and they have no authority over your household. They are not to come and tell you how to run your household and what rules to make for your home. They can make suggestions to you, but you are not obligated to do as they suggest. However, while you are not under their authority, you are under the authority of Christ, and you are obligated to run your household as He says.

When you were a son under the authority of your parents, you had to do as they said. All of your actions and decisions had to meet the approval of your parents. When you got married, you left their authority and came under the authority of Jesus Christ. <u>Now all of your actions and decisions must meet the approval of Jesus Christ</u>. There will never be a time in this life where you will not be under the authority of someone. If you desire a rich and fulfilling marriage, you must acknowledge the authority of Jesus Christ over you, and you must live according to His rules and guidelines.

As a son in your parents' home, you had no one under you that you were to be accountable for. Your parents may have told you to watch over your younger sisters and brothers, but the ultimate responsibility of those children still fell under your parents. As a husband, you have someone under your authority in which you are responsible for. Jesus will hold you accountable as to how you treat your wife and your children. Jesus Christ loves your wife and will deal with you according to how you deal with her. You cannot expect her to yield to your authority if you will not yield to the authority of Christ. Are you striving to yield to the authority of Christ in everything?

7. Leaving ungodly influence

To leave your parents not only means to leave the authority of your parents and come under the authority of Christ, it also means to leave the ungodly influence your parents may have had over you and to come under the influence of Christ. A parent and a child develop certain bonds to each other that cause the parents to still hold influence over their sons (even when those sons are married and have left their parents' home). The mother still holds influence over the son when he refuses to do what most people call _"letting go of mother's apron strings"_. The father may still hold influence over the son by the bad advice and bad examples he imparted into the son, and that son carries them into his marriage. Every husband must be aware of holding on to his mother's apron string, and yielding to the bad advice of the father.

He must be aware of the dangers of allowing his mother to have influence over his marriage, and he must be aware of taking his mother's advice over his wife's advice. You and your wife are now building a life together; she and you are to make every decision, and she and you are to deal with the consequences of those decisions. Do not go to your mother and discuss with her the things that are going on within your home. Never compare your wife with your mother, and do not try to get your wife to do things the way your mother did them. Those things worked in your mother's house, but you are not in your mother's house anymore. Let your wife develop her own way of doing things. Tell your mother you love and respect her, but it is not right nor fair to your wife for your mother to come and try to tell your wife what to do. Respect your mother, love your mother, but keep your mother out of your marriage.

Not only do the apron strings of a mother cause problems in a marriage, but the bad and wrong advice, along with the bad and wrong examples of a father can cause problems in a marriage. We as husbands must come to understand that many of the things our fathers did may still have a negative or positive influence over us. However, we must leave the negative influences of our fathers and seek to come under the influences of Christ through His written Word.

Much of the advice our fathers gave us about marriage may have been wrong according to the Word of God, or they may have been things that may have worked in his home, but they may not work in your homes. Many of the things he did caused problems in his marriage, and they will cause problems in your marriage. If your father told you that you have to slap or hit a woman to keep her in her place, that was wrong advice. If he told you that you shouldn't tell your wife everything you do, that was wrong advice. If you can't tell your wife what you are about to do, don't do it. You are to keep no secrets from your wife, and she is to keep no secrets from you.

If your father told you it is not wrong to have a woman on the side, that was wrong advice. If he told you to never let your wife tell you what to do, that was wrong advice. Your wife can tell you what to do as long as it is in agreement with the Word of God. Our fathers meant well when they gave us this advice, but it was wrong advice that we need to come from under the influence of.

You as a husband need to realize that you are under Christ, and the only advice you are obligated and commanded to obey is that which is found in the Word of God. You need to put much effort into studying the Word of God and applying its teachings and principles into your marriage and life. Only take the advice of your father when it agrees with the commands and teachings found in the Word of God.

Many of the things your fathers may have done in his marriage may have been things that are bad examples for you to follow. You are to only imitate your father as he imitates Jesus Christ. Many of our fathers neglected us, did not participate in the spiritual side of our families, and usually sent us to church instead of taking us. Some fathers did not teach their children to pray nor did they teach them the value of reading and meditating on the Word of God. Many of the things they should have done, mothers had to do. The end result of their bad examples is that we are in danger of making the same mistakes and passing on the same bad examples to our families. Staying out late, drinking, smoking, cursing, and other negative, wrong, and bad actions are examples that you as a husband should not do. When you became a husband, you were to leave your father with his bad advice and examples, and you were to leave your mother with her apron strings, and then come under the influence and authority of Christ.

8. Getting a home of your own for you and your wife

Leaving your father and mother also means to leave their home and get a home of your own for you and your wife. It is not a good thing to marry a woman and then bring her into your father's home to live. You are to establish your own home with your own ways of doing things that you and your wife set up together under the authority of Christ. Your father is the authority in his home (under Christ), and you need to have a home of your own where you can have the authority (under Christ). The home you get does not have to be the biggest nor the best. You may have to start off small and inexpensive, but at least, it will be yours. Every wife feels more comfortable in a home of her own than she will ever feel living with your parents or with her parents. Husbands, for peace sake, and to be obedient to Christ, leave your father and mother and establish a home of your own.

There are times when hardships and unexpected difficulties arise, and you and your family may have to return to your parents' home to live for a while. While there, you are to respect the rules and guidelines your parents have set for their home, while at the same time, seeking to overcome your hardships so you can eventually secure a home of your own. Do not feel bad, inadequate, or as a failure when you must take advantage of the help your parents can give to you. Things happen, and situations arise. That's a part of life. Do not allow bad situations to devastate you; work together with your wife to overcome them.

While you may have to stay with your parents for a season, you will eventually, with the help of God, leave their home and establish a home of your own. If your parents' mental and/or physical health deteriorates to levels where they need you to move in and help them (or other conditions occur), be sure your wife is in agreement with you to move in with your parents before you make a decision to do so. If she does not feel comfortable moving in with your parents, it would be better for you to seek to make other arrangements that will be acceptable to you, your wife, and your parents. Living with your parents is not wrong when you and your spouse are both in agreement to do so.

Father; please work in awesome ways in the hearts and lives of young men so they can learn, receive, and live out the principles found in this book. If they begin right, they can end right. Please place this book into their hands, and then give them a desire to read it. In Jesus' name I pray; amen.

⁹ Wherewithal shall a young man cleanse his way? by taking heed thereto according to thy word. ¹⁰ With my whole heart have I sought thee: O let me not wander from thy commandments. ¹¹ Thy word have I hid in mine heart, that I might not sin against thee. ¹² Blessed art thou, O LORD: teach me thy statutes. (Psalms.119:9-12)

Jesus my LORD; people are destroyed because of a lack of knowledge. I am trusting that the knowledge of Your written Word found in this book will keep young men, middle aged men, and elderly men from being destroyed. Instead of being destroyed, I trust You to cause them to be developed to Your glory.

Jesus is LORD

CHAPTER 9

Uniting as One Flesh with Your Wife

1. The husband is to be joined to his wife, and they are to be one flesh.

2. Being one flesh outside of the marital bond.

3. In marriage, it is God, and not sex that joins two as one flesh. Outside marriage sex joins two as one flesh.

4. Rather with God's choice or your choice, God stilled united you as one flesh.

5. God expects a husband and a wife to receive pleasure in lovemaking just as Sarah received pleasure from her husband Abraham.

6. During the times of physical intimacy in marriage, each should be able to sense the depth of each other's love.

7. God also put sex in marriage to help you and your wife overcome sexual temptations.

8. God also put sex in marriage for reproduction.

9. One life one goal.

10. Husband and wife being one spirit in the sight of God.

11. The husband is to realize that his marriage represents the relationship that Christ has with his church.

12. The priorities of your life as God sees them.

13. The true measure of a man's success in the eyes of God.

1. The husband is to be joined to his wife, and they are to be one flesh.

*³¹ For this cause shall a man leave his father and mother, **<u>and shall be joined unto his wife.</u>** (Ephesians.5:31)*

When a man and a woman unite in holy matrimony, God no longer sees them as two different individuals, but He now sees them as one person and as one flesh. Their two lives have now been woven together is such unity that it's no longer two lives but one life that they now live together. What affects one also affects the other. Every decision is to be for the good of both of them and not just for one in exclusion of the other.

One of the best ways to describe your wife is to say that she is your other self. You can say <u>she is your other self</u> because you and she, in the eyes of God, are united as one spirit and one flesh. You would be correct to tell people you exist in a unified form, your own self and your other self. Your other self is called your wife.

Because your wife has become one with you, you are to treat her with as much love and respect as you treat yourself. You should also be touched with the feelings of her infirmities. To be touched with the feelings of her infirmities means you hurt over what makes her hurt, you rejoice over what makes her rejoice, and you weep over what makes her weep. This occurs because she is you, and you are her.

We, the church, are part of what makes up Christ. Christ is the head, and the church is the body. Your wife is now part of what makes you. She is as much a part of you as your heart and your lungs are a part of you. She, in God's sight, is the bone of your bone and the flesh of your flesh. When you unite in marriage, God does a supernatural thing and unites you and her as one flesh. This uniting as one flesh covers four major areas:

1) The physical side.
2) The sexual side.
3) The life and life goals of the couple.

4) The spiritual side of the couple.

To be one flesh is something God desires for married people only; however, it is possible to be one flesh with someone you are not married to.

*^{15}Know ye not that your bodies are the members of Christ? shall I then take the members of Christ, and make them the members of an harlot? God forbid. ^{16} **What? know ye not that he which is joined to an harlot is one body? for two, saith he, shall be one flesh.** ^{17} But he that is joined unto the Lord is one spirit. ^{18}Flee fornication. Every sin that a man doeth is without the body; but he that committeth fornication sinneth against his own body. (1st Corinthians.6:15-18)*

2. Being one flesh outside of the marital bond

To be one flesh in marriage, however, is totally different from being one flesh outside of the marital bond. To be one flesh to those who are not married is only sexual, and in the eyes of God, it is sinful and defiling. To be one flesh in marriage is holy, godly, and righteous. To be one flesh outside of marriage is unpleasing to God and incurs the wrath of God as well as the judgment of God. To be one flesh within marriage is pleasing to God and causes the couple to receive the blessings of God. To be one flesh outside of marriage causes the sex act to be a defiling sin against one's own body; to be one flesh in marriage causes the sex act (the marriage bed) to be undefiled.

3. In marriage, it is God, and not sex that joins two as one flesh. Outside marriage sex joins two as one flesh

When a couple becomes married, God joints them as one flesh; thus when they engage in sex it is holy, blessed and undefiled. Outside of marriage, sex, not God, joins two as one flesh; thus it is defiling, sinful, and totally displeasing to God.

While being one flesh in marriage includes the sex act, it is not the sex act that makes the married couple one flesh in the sight of God. If a couple were legally married but for some reason have not had sex together, they cannot legally say they are not really married. Whether they have had sex with each other or whether they have not had sex with each other, in the eyes of the law, they are still married. It was not sex that caused them to become married; it was being eligible for marriage and then doing things according to the laws of the state in such ways that they were proclaimed to be husband and wife. If a couple satisfies the conditions of marriage that the state has set forth, they become married (in the eyes of the state) even if they never have sex with each other.

Outside of marriage, the sex act unites two as one physically, but it is a defiling sin against one's own body. Sex is the only thing that unites them. Inside the marital bond, it is not the sex act that unites a couple as one flesh, but it is God that unites them as one flesh. What God has joined together (not what sex as joined together) let no man put asunder (divide or separate).

⁵ And said, For this cause shall a man leave father and mother, and shall cleave to his wife: and they twain shall be one flesh? ⁶· Wherefore they are no more twain, but one flesh. **What therefore God hath joined together,** *let not man put asunder. (Matthew. 19:5-6)*

If you are eligible for marriage according to God's standards and are married in a way acceptable to God, the two of you are made one flesh by God. You and she are one flesh even if you and she have not had sex with each other yet. To be eligible for marriage in the eyes of God, you must not have been married and divorced for a non-biblical reason. Biblical reasons for divorce are adultery, abandonment, and abuse. If you have been divorced for a non-biblical reason and seeks to marry someone else, God sees you as still married to your first spouse; and thus, to remarry would cause you and the person that you are marrying to commit adultery.

⁹ And I say unto you, Whosoever shall put away his wife, except it be for fornication, and shall marry another, **committeth adultery:** *and whoso marrieth her which is put away* **doth commit adultery.** *(Matthew.19:9)*

If you divorced for a non-biblical reason and remarried, but did not know it was wrong in the eyes of God, you can receive grace because of your ignorance (not knowing better).

13. Who was before a blasphemer, and a persecutor, and injurious: **_but I obtained mercy, because I did it ignorantly in unbelief._** *(1ˢᵗ Timothy.1:13)*

Once you realize that it is wrong in God's sight, confess the wrong to God and ask for His forgiveness, and He will forgive you, and He will not see you and your present wife as living in adultery. You can continue with the marriage, and God will bless it.

If a person knows what God says and divorces for a non-biblical reason and then remarries, he and his new spouse are living in adultery. They need to confess that sin to God, asking for His mercy and grace (1ˢᵗ John.1:9-10; 2:1-2). They are not to try to end their present marriage and go back to the previous spouses; they are to seek God for His grace and mercy. You cannot make atonement for the sins of the past, whether they are sins committed out of ignorance or sins committed willfully. Never try to correct the past in this area; just begin living in obedience to God through His written Word and through His Spirit for the present and the future.

4. Rather with God's choice, or your choice, God stilled united you as one flesh

Some people believe that God has a special person He wants them to marry, and if they marry anyone else, they have married the wrong person. They believe that because they did not marry God's choice for them, God does not recognize that marriage, and God did not join them as one flesh. God may have a special person He wants you to marry; however, if you do not marry that person, and you choose to marry someone else, God will still join you and the person you chose as one flesh. It's just that you were joined by God as one flesh with your choice, and not his choice.

Sex in marriage was not the main thing which unites a man and a woman as one flesh. A married couple is first made one flesh in the sight of God, and then they are allowed to have sex with each other. Sex in marriage was given for three main reasons: (1) for pleasure and expressions of emotions of love, (2) for one to resist sin and temptation in sexual areas, and (3) for reproduction of the human race so godly seeds will be born.

5. God expects a husband and a wife to receive pleasure in lovemaking just as Sarah received pleasure from her husband, Abraham.

12. Therefore Sarah laughed within herself, saying, **After I am waxed old shall I have pleasure,** *my lord being old also? (Genesis. 18:12)*

The pleasure of sex in marriage should be fulfilling for both the man and the woman. Husbands, make sure you are doing all you can to sexually satisfy your wife. Don't take the attitude that you got yours (the pleasure you were seeking), and it is up to her to get hers. Always seek to be sure she is as satisfied as you can possibly make her. God expects the lovemaking in marriage to be so emotionally and physically fulfilling, that the husband and the wife get to know each other in deep and personal ways. They should get to know each other in ways that no one else could ever experience with one of them as long as they are both alive.

6. During the times of physical intimacy in marriage, each should be able to sense the depth of each other's love.

Making love should not be a time of physical pleasure only; it should also be a time of expressing deep emotions of love. You should be able to say to your wife by the way you make love to her, that you love her. Self-gratification is sometimes the only thing a husband wants when making love. Husbands, what you should be saying to your wife, by the way you make love to her is, "I want to use the ecstasy of making love to you as part of what I do to show you how deeply I love you." If your wife cannot sense your love for her, when you are making love to her, then you are not really making love to her, because there is no love being shown for her.

Having sex with your wife without expressing emotions of love for her, is not considered making love to her, because you are failing to fulfill one of the major reasons why God put sex in marriage. That major reason is that making love to her, is an opportunity for you to express your undying love for her. Pray asking God to empower you to show your wife you love her when you are making love to her. Without God's help, love making will only be sex. With God's help, love making will be an expression of love that touches your wife's heart.

7. God also put sex in marriage to help you and your wife overcome sexual temptations.

The sex drive in people can be strong and overwhelming at times. Whenever you begin to feel that you can no longer refrain from committing fornication (sex outside of marriage), you are to get married (1st Corinthians.7:2-5). Once married, whenever the desire for sexual fulfillment comes upon you, you are to satisfy that desire with your wife only.

A sad thing that usually happens in a marriage is that when a person is tempted to commit adultery, they yield to the temptation because they know that when they get home, their spouse will probably not want to make love to them. You should live your life in such ways that your wife will know that whenever she is tempted, if she just holds out until she gets home, she can and will get exciting, fulfilling, and wonderful sex from you.

Never leave romance out of the lovemaking process. A woman who commits adultery is usually not looking for sex only, but she is really looking for love and romance. She is looking for someone who will show her that he thinks she is special to him, and for someone who will show her that he loves her. She really wants romance and love more than she wants sex. Husbands, make sure she can find that romance and love in you.

When it comes to sex in your marriage, make it available, make it romantic, make it pleasurable, make it fulfilling, and make it an expression of love. By doing this, you will be helping your wife resist the sexual temptations of adultery that may come her way. If she commits adultery anyway, you will know it is not because you fail to fulfill your part in marriage and love making.

8. God also put sex in marriage for reproduction.

God wants the human race to continue and increase. It is through sex in marriage that God wants this to happen. God is also looking for godly seeds; thus, through sex by married Christian couples, children are born and then raised up in a godly way.

15 And did not he make one? Yet had he the residue of the spirit. And wherefore one? ***That he might seek a godly seed.*** *Therefore take heed to your spirit, and let none deal treacherously against the wife of his youth. (Malachi. 2:15)*

9. One life one goal

To be one flesh in marriage not only includes the sexual side of the marriage; it also includes the life and life goals of the couple. Before marriage, each person had his/her own individual life. When they became united in marriage, it was no longer his life and her life; it became one life now shared together. Before marriage, each had his/her own goals for life; but after marriage, they abandoned their own goals and developed goals they are to accomplish together.

10. Husband and wife being one spirit in the sight of God

Being one flesh is also a spiritual thing that God holds as sacred and holy. God not only looks at them as one physically; He also sees them as one spiritually. In the eyes of God, she has the residue of his spirit (a part of his spirit), and he has the residue of her spirit (a part of her spirit). They are spiritually a part of each other in this life's journey.

¹⁴Yet ye say, Wherefore? Because the LORD hath been witness between thee and the wife of thy youth, against whom thou hast dealt treacherously: yet is she thy companion, and the wife of thy covenant. ¹⁵And did not he make one? **Yet had he the residue of the spirit.** *And wherefore one? That he might seek a godly seed. Therefore take heed to your spirit, and let none deal treacherously against the wife of his youth. ¹⁶For the LORD, the God of Israel, saith that he hateth putting away: for one covereth violence with his garment, saith the LORD of hosts:* **therefore take heed to your spirit,** *that ye deal not treacherously. (Malachi. 2:14-16)*

They are also heirs of the grace of life together.

⁷ Likewise, ye husbands, dwell with them according to knowledge, giving honour unto the wife, as unto the weaker vessel, and **as being heirs together of the grace of life;** *that your prayers be not hindered. (1ˢᵗ Peter. 3:7)*

Because they have a residue of each other's spirit (a part of each other's spirit that God uses to bond them together as one) and are heirs of the grace of life together, God is the only one who can truly separate them. When a couple divorces for a non-biblical reason, they separate the physical part; however, the spiritual part, in God's eyes, is still bonded. When they remarry, they unite the physical part, but the spiritual part is still bonded with the previous spouse because God did not separate them.

God will separate the spiritual side of a marriage only for reasons He gives. He separates the spiritual side at the death of one of the spouses. He separates them for adultery and/or abandonment and/or abuse but only if they get a divorce. If adultery, abandonment, or abuse occurs but the couple decides to stay married and work things out, God does not separate them spiritually.

Husbands, to have a successful marriage, you must realize that you and your wife are one flesh and one spirit in the eyes of God, and only He can separate it. Never seek to live your life for yourself; always keep your wife at the center of all you do. You are her, and she is you; and together, she and you are one.

11. The husband is to realize that his marriage represents the relationship that Christ has with his church.

*³² **This is a great mystery: but I speak concerning Christ and the church.**
(Ephesians. 5:32)*

There is a great mystery concerning marriage that you may not have realized nor considered; however, when this mystery is revealed to you, it has the potential of changing your life and marriage for the better. This mystery will cause you to do things in your marriage that are pleasing to God, and will cause God to bless and prosper every area of your life. It is a mystery God reveals to a person through His Word, and it is a mystery that God desires for all of His married children to apply into their marriage. This mystery is that God wants you to work at making your marriage a reflection of the way Christ treats His bride the church.

The main person responsible for making their marriage a reflection of the way Christ treats His bride, the church, is the husband. Husbands, you are the head of that marriage; and thus, you should be leading the way in treating your wife like Christ treats His church. God instructs your wife to respond to you as she would to Christ; thus, you should be seeking to be as much like Christ as you can be.

One of the reasons many husbands fail to fulfill the mystery of God concerning their marriage is, they are waiting for their wives to become the kind of person they think she should be, before they start treating her like Christ treats His church. They look at what they think are faults and failures within their wives and say, "When she submits to me like the church submits to Christ, then I will treat her as Christ treats His church."

Husbands, you are to treat your wife like Christ treats the church, regardless of how she is acting toward you. In the book of Revelation chapters 2 and 3, Jesus reveals many of the faults that churches have. This lets me know that the church is not perfect, and we have many faults we must overcome. We do not always do as Christ says we should; we often neglect our fellowship time with Christ, and we have not developed into the type of persons Christ wants us to develop into. Regardless of all of that, Jesus still loves us and treats us in grace-filled and wonderful ways. He does not treat us the way we treat Him, nor does He treat us the way we deserve to be treated; He treats us in ways that is much better than we deserve.

12. The priorities of your life as God see them

Should you as a husband become prosperous in every area of life except in the area of treating your wife as Christ treats His church, God looks at your life as a total failure. God sets the priorities of your life in this order:

1) Your relationship with Himself through His son Jesus Christ.
2) Your relationship with your wife and children.
3) Your relationship with other people.
4) Your work for Christ.
5) Your career.
6) All your other relationships.

If you fail in the first two priorities, God sees the rest of your life as a total failure.

Many husbands are doing well in their careers, in their relationships with others, and in church work; but their personal time with Christ is lacking, and their relationship with their wife and family is hurting. These husbands usually do not pray as they should and only study the Bible when they have to teach it to others. They do not study just to get to know God better and to become a better person. These husbands also are failing to treat their wives as Christ treats the church, and they are failing to raise their children in the nurture and admonition of the Lord.

4. And, ye fathers, provoke not your children to wrath: **_but bring them up in the nurture and admonition of the Lord._** *(Ephesians.6:4)*

These husbands spend more time developing their careers than they do developing their relationship with Christ and their relationship with their wives. These husbands oftentimes treat other people with more respect than they do their wives. They speak pleasantly to people at work, in stores, and in other places; but they snap at their wives. While they say good morning to people at work and hold beautiful conversations with them, they will wake up in the morning and say nothing to their wives and usually hold no conversation with her during the day. They will give the common courtesies of life to others, but they will not give them to their wives.

Husbands, if you do not treat your wife better than you treat other people, you are not treating her as Christ would have you to treat her. Jesus treats no one better than He treats His church. Jesus treats no one as good as He treats His church. Husbands, to make your marriage a reflection of Christ and His church, you must be like Christ and treat your wife better than you treat everyone else and anything else.

Many husbands are doing exceptional jobs at church but are doing horrible jobs at home. They act like mighty men of faith and power, and they hold prominent positions in the church. But their marriages are falling apart, and it is their fault. It is their fault because they fail to treat their wives as Christ treats His church. They complain that their wives are not right when in reality they are the ones who are not right. They are not right because they are not treating her like Christ treats His church. God is not impressed with the amount of energy and effort they put into other areas of life, if they are not putting more energy and effort into the two major priorities of life that He has set for them. Those two major priorities are (1) his personal relationship with God through Jesus Christ and (2) his relationship with his wife and family.

13. The true measure of a man's success in the eyes of God

God does not measure a man's level of success by such things as how much money he makes, how well he does in his career, and how well his relationship with others outside his home is going. Nor does God measure a man's success solely on how he performs in his church work and in his Christian service. God measures success for a man on how well he maintains his relationship with God and on how well he is fulfilling the great mystery of God in treating his wife like Christ treats His church. Only after he shows great effort to succeed in those two areas of life does God begin considering rewarding him in other areas of life.

Father; in these last days, You need saved husbands and men who will love You, trust You, pray to You, worship You, and be used of You to defeat the forces of darkness. Husbands and men who will be mighty men of valor and powerful soldiers in Your army. Thank You for anointing us to be vessels of honor sanctified and fit for Your use, to Your glory. In Jesus' name I pray; amen.

^{21}If a man therefore purge himself from these, he shall be a vessel unto honour, sanctified, and meet for the master's use, and prepared unto every good work. (2nd Timothy.2:21)

Jesus my LORD; as times, people, and this world becomes worse and worse; Your husbands and men must become better and better. We must increase in love, developed in righteousness, and advance in dominion. We must shine as bright lights, fight as mighty soldiers, and preach like powerful prophets. By the power of the Holy Ghost we purpose to be these things and more to Your glory.

Jesus is LORD

CHAPTER 10

Guarding Against Bitterness

1. The power of repetition.

2. The Husband is to love his wife.

3. The husband is not to be bitter toward his wife.

4. Reasons why bitterness comes into a man's heart.

5. Overcoming Bitterness Because of Adultery.

6. You must forgive.

7. Beware not to commit the same sin of adultery.

8. Forgive, forget, and don't hold it over her head.

9. Regaining trust and lost emotions.

10. Bitterness without a Cause.

11. Overcoming having bitterness without a cause.

12. Bitterness because of past hurts.

13. Bitterness because of wrong information.

14. Bitterness because of sin.

1. The power of repetition

*¹² Wherefore **I will not be negligent to put you always in remembrance of these things, though ye know them,** and be established in the present truth.*

*¹³ Yea, I think it meet, as long as I am in this tabernacle, **to stir you up by putting you in remembrance;** (2ⁿᵈ Peter.1:12-13)*

*⁵ **I will therefore put you in remembrance, though ye once knew this,** how that the Lord, having saved the people out of the land of Egypt, afterward destroyed them that believed not. (Jude.1:5)*

Throughout the Holy Bible, God constantly repeats something in one passage of scripture that He has already said in another passage of scripture. The reason He does this is because some people do not read the entire Bible, and if God did not repeat Himself, they would miss something He wants them to know. Another reason why God repeats Himself is because He knows many of us do not always gain understanding the first time around. Because we do not gain proper understanding the first time, God has to repeat Himself and further expound on something He has said. One passage may magnify and expound on something that was mentioned in another passage.

God also repeats Himself when there is something of great importance He wants to impart within His children. In the mouth of two or three witnesses, every word is to be established. God uses two or more passages so that the words He speaks will be totally established within the hearts of the believers. We as children of God should learn to apply this method of God in our teaching process. This method is applied when a person repeats principles and teachings he has taught earlier.

When parents are trying to instill Christian values within their children, repetition is not a boring thing, but it is a needed tool that will help children learn and remember the principles and teachings that the parents are seeking to teach them. They learn the words to a song not by writing down the words and studying them, but by hearing the words again and again. Christian children can also learn and remember godly principles and teachings by hearing them repeatedly.

As we advance in our study on God's Divine instructions to husband and men, you will notice that what God says in one passage, He will repeat in another. In Ephesians.5:25 God command men to love their wives. Now, in Colossians.3:19, He is repeating the same command for men to love their wives. The command for men to love their wives is so important to God that He constantly repeats it throughout scripture.

2. The husband is to love his wife.

[19] Husbands, love your wives. (Colossian. 3:19)

God instructing husbands to love their wives is a repeat of the principle He taught in Ephesians 5:25, 28, and 33. This principle is so important to God that He repeats it again and again within His Word. Because of this repetition, husbands have no excuse for not knowing they are commanded by God to love their wives. Husbands, loving your wife is one of the main priorities God sets for a husband and is a principle you should strive with all your heart to fulfill. For information on how a husband is to love his wife, you may refer again to the section of this book entitled the husband is to love his wife like Christ loves the church" (Ephesians. 5:25). In that section of this book, there is detailed information on what love is, and on how a husband is to love his wife like Christ loves the church.

If you as a husband want to learn to love your wife, there are certain passages and books in the Holy Bible you will need to study. You will need to study 1st Corinthians 13:1-8. In that passage of scripture, there are great principles of love that will help you learn how to love your wife as God instructs you to; (in this passage of scripture the word *charity* is an old English word which can be translated into the word *love*). How intensely you study that passage will reveal how intensely you want to obey God and how intensely you want to love your wife.

To learn to love your wife as God instructs, you must also study the Song of Solomon. In studying the Song of Solomon, you will learn how to love your wife in a romantic and fulfilling way. This book talks about how a man is to pursue his wife romantically and how he is to always give her compliments. It reveals how his wife is to be all fair and lovely to him and is to be the only love of his life. This book is one of the most beautiful love stories ever written, and its interpretation reveals Christ's love for His church. Compare the way you romantically treat your wife to the Song of Solomon, and if you are not doing as he is doing, you are falling short in the loving your wife department.

Husbands, you must come to realize how important it is for you to love your wife in the right way and how to show that love. The most important thing in all existence is love. God himself is love (1st John 4:8,16). Because God is love, He will accept nothing less than you loving your wife.

3. The husband is not to be bitter toward his wife.

^{19} *Husbands, love your wives,* ***and be not bitter against them.*** *(Colossians. 3:19)*

In Hebrews 12:14-15, God tells Christians to diligently follow peace and holiness because if we do not, a root of bitterness may spring up in us, and many may be defiled. One of the reasons many marriages are destroyed is because of a root of bitterness that springs up in one or both spouses, and that bitterness defiled and eventually destroyed that marriage. Husbands, in order to guard against the defilement and possible destruction of your marriage because of bitterness, God firmly commands you to not be bitter toward your wives.

There are some dangerous things that can happen in a marriage that can cause a husband to become bitter toward his wife, and thus disobey the instruction of God for husbands not to be bitter toward their wives. These things can bring so much pain to him that it may cause him to become bitter toward his wife and react to her in negative ways. Because of bitterness, he may react to her by (1) becoming an angry person toward her and/or (2) by developing an attitude of apathy toward her and/or (3) by committing adultery. Husbands, beware of the things that can cause a root of bitterness to spring up in you; and if things happen that have the potential to incite bitterness, learn to react in the right way, and learn to work to overcome those things.

4. Reasons why bitterness comes into a man's heart

While there are many things that can cause a root of bitterness to spring up in a man, there are five causes that usually happen the most, hurt the deepest, and are the hardest to overcome. These five things are:

1) Realizing your wife does not love you as a wife should love her husband.
2) Knowing that you cannot satisfy your wife sexually.
3) Discovering that your wife is being unfaithful to you.
4) Seeing that your wife has lost all respect for you, and looks at you as being no better than any other person.

Realizing your wife does not submit to you nor to your authority (she does things you ask her not to, and she does not do things you ask her to).

When one or more of these things happen, a husband may feel demoralized and less than a man. These are also things that can be used by the devil to cause a husband to become a bitter person and react in many sinful ways. Many husbands are angry with their wives because of one or more of these reasons. Many husbands speak harshly to their wives and mistreat their wives because of one or more of these things. Many husbands have developed an attitude of indifference and apathy toward their wives, and some husbands are even involved in an adulterous relationship because of one or more of those things. These things are dangerous, deadly, and defiling. Thus, husbands, you must learn to deal with them properly; or they may destroy your marriage.

When a wife commits one or more of these things, especially adultery, it hurts her husband so badly that he may want to react in anger and violence. He feels he cannot control himself, and may want to give in to anger at the moment. You as a husband must always make it your prime goal never to resort to violence toward your wife. God says it's alright to be angry but sin not, even if the anger is prompted by adultery. Get away from her for a while, cry if you must, yell if you must, but never hit and never abuse her.

To react in a sinful way will be hurtful to you, to your wife, and to your marriage. To overcome those five dangerous things, you as a husband must realize it is not her actions that carries the most weight, but it is your reactions that will carry the most weight. Also, realize you have a choice of how you will react. You can choose to react in bitterness or choose to react according to the Word of God. You will hurt because of those things; but be a man, bear the pain, and react according to God's Word and will.

To avoid developing a root of bitterness toward your wife, be very sensitive to the way you treat her on a regular basis, and keep the lines of communication open. Also, develop an attitude that regardless of what problems may come into your marriage, you will seek to always work to overcome them, and you will try to make your marriage into the type of marriage God desires marriages to be.

I am a firm believer that problems come to strengthen us and give us something to overcome. The lack of love, the lack of respect, and the lack of sexual fulfillment are not reasons to become bitter and to end the marriage; they are signs that reveal a challenge to improve yourself, your wife, and your marriage. When problems and difficulties come, it is not time to give up nor is it time to end the marriage. It is a time to do things differently and to do things that will help to bring victory. The things that will help to bring victory are showing love, strength, courage, and working diligently to overcome these challenges.

5. Overcoming bitterness because of adultery

If your wife was to commit adultery, it would so devastate you that it would become one of the hardest things for you to overcome. The pain runs so deep that reconciliation seems impossible. You will feel you can never forgive her, and you may want to end the marriage. Your first reaction, however, should be to cry out to God, asking Him to help you deal with the pain and to react according to His will. Next, set aside some time alone for prayer and for meditation, but do not allow yourself to dwell on the evil thoughts the devil will bring your way. Tell God of your pain and that you need Him to help you heal. Tell God that you do not want to forgive her and that you need His help to open up your heart to forgiveness.

6. You must forgive

Whatever you decide to do, part of it will have to include forgiveness. You will never justify before God a heart of un-forgiveness. Even if you decide to divorce, you will still be required of God to forgive her. Forgiveness is something you can't get around. It is something you must do. Begin now by asking for God's help in that area. Also, remember you need God's forgiveness just as your wife needs your forgiveness. There were sins you committed against God that you needed Him to forgive you of. For Jesus to bring forgiveness to you cost Him more than what it will cost you to forgive your wife. If you want God to forgive you, you must forgive your wife.

[25] And when ye stand praying, forgive, if ye have ought against any: that your Father also which is in heaven may forgive you your trespasses. [26] **_But if ye do not forgive, neither will your Father which is in heaven forgive your trespasses._** *(Mark 11:25-26)*

Not only do you need God's forgiveness, many husbands also need their wives to forgive them for committing the same sin they have committed. Many men have been unfaithful to their wives, and their wives may not have known it. How can you hold against her something you have done yourself? Whether she knows what you have done or not, you did it; and it is time for you to forgive her, and for her to forgive you. After you have forgiven her, it will be time for you and your wife to figure out what she and you are going to do. In trying to figure out what to do, you need to first seek spiritual counseling from your pastor. It is not time to do things alone; you will need some spiritual help from others. When seeking help from others, use caution and be discreet. Confide in as few people as possible, and only those who are helping you deal with the problem.

7. Beware not to commit the same sin of adultery

Husbands, do not confide in nor tell another woman (whom you are friends with), what your wife has done. Do not become intimate friends with other women. You do not need to be around them, and you do not need them to console you. Do not go and try to get even with your wife by committing adultery yourself. For you to commit adultery will be a sin against yourself and a sin against your God; and it will only make things worse. Remember it was adultery that caused the hurts, and problems you are now in, so do not try to use what created the problems to try to solve the problems.

When seeking to figure out what to do, try to make reconciliation one of your major choices. For reconciliation to come between you and her, you must be willing to offer it to her, and she must be willing to repent of her sins. Your wife will have to confess her sins to God. She will also have to make up her mind that she will never commit adultery again. She, then, must be willing to work to regain your trust and to rebuild your love.

8. Forgive, forget, and don't hold it over her head

If you and she decide to stay together and work the problem out, do not make it hard on her by constantly bringing up the subject. You and she will also have to work together to keep unfaithfulness from happening again in your marriage. You are not to keep holding her sins and mistakes over her head. Because you and she have decided to go on in life together, you need to live your life in such a way that she will know that while you may not be able to erase her sins from your memory, you are not holding it against her and you are forgiving her. Never develop the mentality that she must constantly do things to make it up to you.

Once you have forgiven her, work on forgetting also. To forget does not mean you will erase it from your memory. To forget means although it happened, you will go forward in life, you will learn from it, and you will treat your wife as if it never happened. Love overcomes all adversities; thus, you must continue to love her, respect her, and treat her as a husband should treat his wife. While this may seem a difficult task, it is a task that must be done.

It will take much time, prayer, and patience. You will have to control your thoughts, and you are not to continually confront your wife nor question your wife about the affair.

Rebuilding a marriage after there has been unfaithfulness is a challenge that can be done. The question is not, "Can it be done?" The question is, "Are you and she willing to do it?" You can do all things through Christ who strengthens you, that is, if you want to do it.

9. Regaining trust and lost emotions

Trying to regain trust and recapture lost emotions will be a task that both you and she will have to work diligently to accomplish. It will take time, and it will take much effort. It will be hard, but in time, it can be done. Unfaithfulness is a disaster that causes much destruction in a marriage; but forgiveness, prayer, patience, love, and hard work make up the construction cure you and God will use to rebuild the damaged marriage.

10. Bitterness Without a Cause

Some men are bitter toward their wives even when their wives have not done anything wrong. These husbands hold a root of bitterness because (1) they are bitter by nature; (2) they were hurt in the past; (3) they just never learned how to love the Christ kind of way; (4) they have been preprogrammed with false information about how to treat a wife; (5) they are afraid of being hurt, so they try to guard themselves against it; and (6) they are involved in sins such as alcohol, drugs, adultery, gambling, etc.

Many women are living in a nightmare of a marriage because their husbands are bitter against them when they have done nothing to cause that bitterness. All they have tried to do to get their husbands to cease having bitterness toward them have failed, and they are on the verge of leaving. They are unhappy, and their children are unhappy. They and their children feel they are in bondage, and it is all because of their husband's and father's bitterness. One of the hardest things to deal with is someone you love being bitter against you without a cause, and there seems to be nothing you can do to cause that bitterness to cease.

11. Overcoming having bitterness without a cause

Some men are bitter by nature and have never tried to overcome their bitter nature. They are easily angered and vent their anger on their wives. If you are a Christian man and you are bitter against your wife, you are in sin; you are not loving her like Christ loves the church, and you are making your home less than it should be. You must make up your mind that you will turn your bitterness into love and tenderness. Bitterness is not a quality Christ possesses, and it should not be a quality you possess. Bitterness is a destructive force that slowly erodes the foundation of a marriage. Husbands, you must come to realize what bitterness is doing to you and to your marriage, and then you must repent of that bitterness. Learn to abandon bitterness by embracing actions of love, romance, and appreciation toward your spouse.

To turn from your bitterness, you need to confess to yourself and to your God that you harbor bitterness within you. Ask your wife to forgive you, and make her a promise that you will do all you can to stop being bitter against her. Also, you must always pray, asking God to help you turn from the attitude of bitterness that you have toward her. You must also be renewed in your mind by reading and studying the holy Word of God. Learn to exercise patience with your wife, and work to allow nothing to cause you to be neither angry nor bitter against her.

Along with those things, you need to start showing wonderful acts of love toward her regularly and continually. It is hard and even impossible to express two opposite types of emotions at the same time (you cannot be sad and happy, bitter and loving, angry and joyful all at the same time). If you are busy always expressing emotions of love, you will not have time nor space in your heart to express emotions of bitterness. When you find yourself getting bitter against her, purposely do something sweet and nice for her that will show you love her. After showing acts of love and kindness, sit down and talk to your wife about the fact that you are a bitter person, and then discuss with her ways you and she can overcome it. Open communication between you and her will be a powerful tool you both can use to help overcome your bitterness.

When talking to your wife, inform her of the things she does that usually cause you to react bitterly toward her, then suggest to her a different way of doing those things. Let her know it is not because she is doing something wrong, but you have not gotten to the point where you can totally deal with your emotions of bitterness, and you need her help. Many times, however, you must allow your wife to do things her way; and when you feel emotions of bitterness coming up, you are not to stop your wife from doing what she is doing; you are to stop yourself from being bitter. Self-control is a must when it comes to properly dealing with bitterness.

12. Bitterness Because of Past Hurts

Many men have deep emotional hurts within them because of things that happened in the past. Because of these hurts, they have developed a root of bitterness, and it is displayed toward their wives. Being abandoned by their fathers, rejected by friends, being rejected by loved ones, having feelings of not measuring up to the standards of others (or their own standards), and other negative things that happened to them are all contributing factors to them becoming a bitter person.

Although their wives have done nothing to hurt them, they usually are the ones who receive the brunt of their husbands' bitterness. Misplaced attitudes of bitterness are just as destructive as misplaced anger.

You should never allow the hurts of the past to interfere with your today and to destroy your tomorrows. Past hurts are to be dealt with and overcome by recognizing them, confronting them, and getting rid of them. Men have a tendency to suppress negative emotions instead of dealing with them. If you are a husband who holds bitterness within your heart, you need to admit that you are a bitter person, and then try to find out the real cause of your bitterness. The cause of your bitterness is not your wife, but it may be something that hurt you in the past.

To find the true source of your bitterness, you need to begin with prayer to God, asking Him to reveal it to you. You may need to be alone so you can think and meditate on events of the past. Be honest with yourself, and be willing to confront the things that have happened in the past that you hated. What things are there that you would change about your past if you knew you could change them? Those things you would change are probably some of the things that caused your hurt and your bitterness. The events of the past will hurt again as you think of them, but these are thoughts that you must face if you are going to deal with them and overcome your bitterness.

Once you recognize the source of your bitterness, you must forgive the one(s) who caused your hurts, especially if that person is yourself. Then determine that you will not allow yourself to hurt others as others have hurt you. Instead of being the cause of others living in misery, be determined to cause others to live in joy and happiness because of the things you do for them.

If you are bitter because of many past failures and because of falling short of your (and others') expectations, you need to realize that those expectations may not have been God's goals for your life. Also, realize while you may have fallen short in the eyes of others, you have not fallen short in the eyes of God. God knew you would be where you are now, and He has plans for your life that starts from where you are now and will carry you to where He wants you to be. You have a choice to make; you can allow the past to rob your future, or you can start today to build a future of joy and love with what you have, and from where you are now. The hurts of the past were sad and terrible, but to allow them to destroy your present and your future is tragic.

13. Bitterness Because of Wrong Information

Many men have been preprogrammed with false information about how to treat a wife; thus, they react to their wives in wrong ways, and one of those wrong ways is reacting bitterly toward her. Men were told they had to be strong and firm with a woman because if they did not, she would walk all over them. Men often make the mistake of interpreting being strong and firm as being bitter. Jesus is not described as strong and firm when it comes to dealing with His bride, the church. He is described as being loving, merciful, and kindhearted. Jesus shows tender mercy and loving kindness to us; and we, the church, do not walk all over Him. Instead of trying to walk all over Him, we seek to reverence Him, love Him, and obey Him.

If you are treating your wife in any other way than in love, you are treating her wrong. If you want your wife to reverence you, love you, and obey you, get rid of the bitterness and be a man of tender mercy and loving kindness toward her. God tells us that our wives are the weaker vessels. You do not deal with weak vessels with a strong hand and a firm grip; you deal with them with tender loving care.

Many of the things men were told about dealing with women have caused the wreck and ruin of many marriages. Husbands, oftentimes, we must abandon the erroneous advice of our fathers and other men, and we must take the advice found in the Word of God. Our father's advice did not work too well in their marriages, and it will not work in ours. Ask your mother, and she can tell you ways that she wishes her husband would change. She will tell you of the years when she lived in dissatisfaction and only stayed married for the children's sake.

Your mother can tell you of the nights of loneliness, sadness, and tears. She can tell you of the times when her love for her husband had diminished into nothing. Then she will tell you what to do and what never to do when dealing with your wife. She can tell you the type of man she wishes her husband was to her and the type of man she wishes you were to your wife. As she tells you the type of man to be, you will notice that it is the type of man Jesus is, and the type of man God tells you to be.

Not all fathers give bad advice; many gave good advice on how to treat a wife. The way you can determine what good advice is, is if the advice lines up with the written Word of God. Good advice is an advice that causes a wife to love her husband more and become a better wife for him. It is also advice that makes him a better and godlier person. One day, it may be time for you to give advice to your sons on how to treat a wife. Let your advice be the best type of advice. The best type of advice is godly advice that is lived out at home as an example to them. God's Word works, and it will work for you and for your sons.

14. Bitterness Because of Sin

Sin is a hideous thing that brings misery and suffering into the lives of people. Sin is the one thing that keeps God's children from acting the way He wants them to act. Sin has the ability to alter a person's attitude and causes him to react in a fashion that is contrary to God's Word and will. Sin will cause you to love what you should hate and hate what you should love. If you are involved in sin, you are showing hatred to the ones you should love and showing love to the ones you probably should not be around. Your attitude has been altered, and you are not acting as God would have you to act.

Sin has the innate ability to bring the worst out in a person, and it has an uncanny way of bringing out bitterness in a husband. When you are involved in sin, if you could notice the change in your personality and attitude, you would realize that you are starting to act bitterly toward your wife. You will also notice that regardless of what she does, it still just is not right to you. The problem is not her, and the problem is not the way she does things; the problem is what sin is doing to you. Sin is deceiving you, and it is destroying you and your marriage. If you were to repent of the sin, you would notice how much better you and your wife would get along. You will notice how your love for your wife is increasing, and for some reason, she now does things in a way that is favorable to you. It was not that your wife changed; it was that you got rid of your sin and sin's negative effects within you and your life.

Bitterness is a devastating tool of the devil that God warns husbands to stay away from. It is a major force in destroying marriages, and it leads to discouragement and disaster. It causes those who are supposed to be united as one, to act like mortal enemies. Bitterness is a defiling and destructive tool of the devil that seems to work every time when it comes to destroying marriages. To overcome the dangerous and the damning power of bitterness, God gives husbands the perfect key to use. That key is, "Husbands, love your wives and be not bitter toward them."

*[19] Husbands, love your wives, **and be not bitter against them.** (Colossians. 3:19)*

Father; when I think about the awesomeness of who You are, I don't have time to be bitter. When I think about how much You love me, I don't have time to be bitter. When I think about how much You daily bless me, I don't have time to be bitter. The greatest weapon I have to overcome and destroy bitterness is You. the joy of You is my strength. In Jesus' name I pray; amen.

*[10]Then he said unto them, Go your way, eat the fat, and drink the sweet, and send portions unto them for whom nothing is prepared: for this day is holy unto our Lord: neither be ye sorry; **for the joy of the LORD is your strength.** (Nehemiah.8:10).*

Jesus my LORD; thank You for giving me Your joy. Because of Your joy in me, my Joy is full. Instead of becoming overwhelmed with the bitterness of satan, I will become overshadowed with your joy.

[11]These things have I spoken unto you, that my joy might remain in you, and that your joy might be full. (John.15:11)

Jesus is LORD

CHAPTER 11

Dwelling with Your Wife according to Knowledge

1. The husband is to dwell with his wife according to knowledge.

2. Husbands must study the Word of God.

3. As life and circumstances change, you must change in the way you treat your wife.

4. Husbands, do not harden your heart to the Word of God.

5. The consequences of disobeying God's Word.

6. Dwelling with your wife according to the knowledge of the things you have learned about her.

7. Learning things about your wife that she has not told you of.

8. Trial and error does work.

9. Verbal communication.

10. Romance, understanding, and tender loving care.

11. Your wife is intelligent.

12. Give her some space at times.

God's Divine Instructions To Husbands and Men

1. The husband is to dwell with his wife according to knowledge

*7 Likewise, ye husbands, **dwell with them according to knowledge.** (1st Peter. 3:7)*

When God tells you as a husband to dwell with your wife according to knowledge, there are two basic areas He is referring to. God wants you to dwell with her according to the knowledge He has given you in His written Word about how to treat a wife. God also wants you to dwell with her according to the things you have learned about her. If you do not know what God says about women, wives, marriage, and your duties concerning them, you will be lacking as a husband. If you do not know your wife's likes and dislikes, habits and ways of doing things, moods and mood changes, along with certain other intimate things about her, you will be in trouble as a husband.

Many husbands either fail in marriage, or have a hard time in marriage because they do not do what God tells them to do concerning their wives. The reasons they do not do as God says are;

A. Because they do not know what God says, so they can't do it;
B. Because of the hardness of their hearts, they refuse to do it;
C. Because they think they have a better way than God's way, they do not do as God says.

Instead of doing as God says in His written Word, they try to do things their own way. To violate God's Word will always bring problems and hardships upon those violating it, and it also will bring problems and hardships to others. The majority of the problems couples confront in their marriages are a result of the husband, the wife, or both violating the commands and instructions of God.

2. Husbands must study the Word of God

Every husband should take time out to study

1. What God says in His Word about marriage
2. What God says in His Word about men and husbands
3. What God says in His Word about women and wives

Not knowing these things may cause marriages to end in divorce, or it may cause marriages to never be all they could be. Not knowing these things can prevent a husband from being the type of man and husband God wants him to be, and/or it may cause him to never treat his wife right (treat her in a way that is according to the Word of God). Not knowing these things can cause a husband to never truly understand his wife, and it can cause him to not be the type of husband she desires for him to be. When it comes to developing a successful marriage, constantly studying and obeying the Word of God is something every husband must do.

Husbands often make terrible mistakes and do things that really hurt their wives. They do these things and make these mistakes because they ignorantly violated the Word of God. There are certain things God tells husbands to do, but many husband make the mistake of not doing those things. When a husband fails to do as God instructs in His Word, it usually leaves their wives hurt and unfulfilled. Not only do many husbands fail to do what God says to do, they often end up doing things God tells them not to do. When they do things God tells them not to do, their actions of disobedience to God causes problems between them and their spouse. After the damage is done, they wonder what is wrong and why their wives are not happy. If these husbands had been studying the Word of God, they would know what the problem is, and they would know how to correct it.

3. As life and circumstances change, you must change in the way you treat your wife

As you study the Word of God to learn what He says about marriage, husbands, and wives, you will realize that it will be a lifelong study. You will not learn everything at one time. As you and your wife live together, you both will go through different stages in life. Each stage of life will cause you to deal with her in different ways. You do not deal with your wife after she goes through menopause the same way you did before she went through menopause. You can't expect your wife to deal with you the same way after she has children as she did before she had children. She will not have the time or energy to give you the amount of attention she gave you before the children came.

Life changes, people change, circumstances change, and you too will go through changes. As these changes occur and different stages of life come, God will teach you during each stage how to deal with them. If you fail to learn the lessons of the different stages of life that God teaches you, it will cause great problems for you and your wife. To complain that your wife is changing when it is natural for her to change will cause problems. Do not expect her to always be the same; she will change, and so will you.

The problem is not the changes in life that occur; the problem is you not knowing how to deal with those changes when they occur. As you study the Word of God, God will reveal unto you that young women are in a learning stage while the older women are in their teaching stage (Titus 2:3-5). He will reveal to you that when you were a young man, you were a strong warrior in life; but as an older man, you are no longer for war but for counsel. You will learn from the Word that young men have great visions while older men experience great dreams (Acts 2:17). The proper way to deal with the different changes and stages of life is taught only in the Word of God.

Along with studying the Word of God, also seek to learn from the wisdom God has given to other godly men. Read books, listen to sermons, attend men's conferences, and do other things of that nature that will help you learn and grow. Talk to aged godly men who have the wisdom of knowing how to build a successful marriage. If you want your marriage to be all it can be, you must major in studying the Word of God throughout your life, you must learn what proper changes you must make as life change, and you must get wisdom and advice from wise godly men who possess a good and successful marriage.

4. Husbands, do not harden your heart to the Word of God

It usually is not the part of the Holy Bible you do not know that causes the greatest problems; it is the part you know but fail to obey that usually causes the greatest problems. Wives know they are to submit to their husbands; however, when they do not submit, problems come. Most men know they are to love their wives like Christ loves the church; however, when they do not love her that way, problems come. God says to give the tithe and offerings, but we don't give as God says; thus, problems come. When you know to do good but don't do it, it is sin, and it will cause problems for you. God has given us His Word to aid us in avoiding many of the problems and pitfalls that can occur in life; thus, it is of great importance for every Christian couple to learn and obey the written Word of God.

Have you hardened your heart when it comes to the Word of God? Have you hardened your heart by not reading it regularly? Many men harden their hearts when it comes to reading the Bible. They will read the newspaper, they will read magazines, they will read books; but they will not read their Bibles. They will work on their cars, they will work on their homes, they will work on their yards; but they will not work at reading their Bibles. They will do this, they will do that, they will do the other; but they will not read their Bibles. If you are a man who will not read your Bible, you are a hard-hearted man who is on his way to big trouble.

5. The consequences of disobeying God's Word

Not only do men often harden their hearts to reading the Bible, they, at times, also harden their hearts to obeying it. Husbands can be so hard-hearted at times that it can cause our wives to say we are just being downright stubborn. Our hard-hearted stubbornness in not obeying the Word of God is the most dangerous thing we can do. It causes trouble in our marriages and problems in our lives. It also angers God.

1. When we, the children of God, violate the Word of God, it causes God to get involved in our lives to chasten us into correction. (Hebrews.12:5-11)
2. When we violate the Word of God, it allows the devil to become involved in our lives to destroy us. (Ephesians.4:27)

If you were to review the times in your life when you suffered great problems and difficulties, you will find that the majority of those problems and difficulties came because you did something in violation of God's Word.

God is merciful and long-suffering, but he will not allow his children to constantly sin. If there is continual sin in your life, it will cause God to turn you over to the devil for the destruction of the flesh so the spirit may be saved in the day of judgment. (1st Corinthians 5:4-5; 1st Timothy. 1:20). Sin may allow the devil to kill you. To be killed by the devil because of sin does not only mean to take your life; it can also mean to kill your finances, your physical health, your mental health, your joy, your peace, your prosperity, your family relationship, and a host of other horrible things that can happen.

Not only does sin allow the devil to come in to kill, steal, and destroy; it may cause God to chasten you. To be chastened means to cause one to correct their wrong behavior because God allows unpleasant things to happen. These things will happen in such ways that it will prompt a person to repent of their sins and begin doing works of righteousness (doing things that are right in the sight of God) (Hebrews.12:5-11). The difference between God's chastening and the devil's destruction is the devil is trying to totally destroy a person and leave them unable to recover. God is trying to get a person to stop doing their wrong and begin doing right. **God seeks to correct; the devil seeks to destroy.**

God will first chasten you before He allows the devil to destroy you. If the things God does in your life will not cause you to repent, God will allow the devil to come in, and the devil will seek to destroy you. The devil has destroyed many marriages because many husbands would not repent at the chastening of God. They heard God's voice telling them the right things to do, but they hardened their hearts. God allowed many unpleasant things to happen in an attempt to get them to repent, but they hardened their hearts to it. They knew they should have repented, but they hardened their hearts to it. After hardening their hearts for so long, the devil came in with destruction.

Are you in the midst of God chastening you? Are you hearing the voice of God telling you to repent and start doing things His way? Are unpleasant things now happening in your life? If you love yourself, if you love your wife, if you love your God; please repent now because if you don't, the devil will come in to destroy.

Not all bad and unpleasant things that happen in your life happen as a result of sin. God is not always trying to chasten you when bad things happen. You may be living right as best as you can, and you may not be involved in any known sin, but unpleasant things may still happen. These unpleasant things happen because there are times when the devil will attack you and your life when you have done nothing sinful to merit these attacks. When the devil attacks and there is no known sin within your life, it is not time for repentance; it is time to fight against the devil and his works.

The way you can tell the attack of the devil from the chastening of God is if you have not hardened your heart to the Word of God, then it is not God's chastening; is the devil attacking. When the devil attacks, make sure you have on the whole armor of God (Ephesians.6:10-18), and then take the weapons of your warfare (2nd Corinthians.10:4-6) and defeat him.

God stops chastening when you rid yourself of your hardened heartens, repent of your sins, and begin doing works of righteousness (begin doing things God's way). The devil stops attacking when you stand against him and defeat him with prayer, faith, the Word of God, and the name of Jesus Christ.

6. Dwelling with your wife according to the knowledge of the things you have learned about her

Men often make great quests to gain knowledge and understanding. Men make dangerous journeys through the mountains and forests of distant countries in search of some mysterious hidden knowledge. Men will spend tens of thousands of dollars on higher education in order to acquire wisdom, knowledge, and understanding. Much energy and effort is expended, much money and resources are spent, and many years of study are given in their quest for knowledge. After doing all of that, it is hard to understand why we do such stupid stuff when it comes to our wives.

You need to study your wife to learn her likes and dislikes. You need to learn her habits and her ways of doing things. The study course on your wife is a study course that you are required to take, it is a study course that will last a lifetime, and it is a study course in which you will never graduate. When you think you have learned all there is to learn about her, she will do something that will let you know you haven't learned anything yet.

When studying your wife, don't expect her to tell you everything you need to know. Oftentimes, a wife expects her husband to know things about her that she has never told him. She feels that after so many years of marriage, there are things he should just know; and if he does not know those things, it is because he does not love her. The problem is not a problem of him not loving her; it is just that he has failed to study her so that he can live with her according to knowledge; or that she has just went through some kind of unexpected change that he has had no time to adjust to.

7. Learning things about your wife that she has not told you of.

To learn things about your wife that she has not told you, notice all she does, try the trial and error method, and notice how she reacts to certain things you do. Also, when studying your wife so you can dwell with her according to knowledge, expect her likes and dislikes to change; and expect her routines and habits to change as well. If you fail to learn that your wife will change, you have failed a major part of the course on the study of your wife.

By seeking to notice all you can about your wife, you will learn many important things. If she keeps a clean house, you will learn you should never leave your clothes and things lying around all over the place; you will learn that she expects you to make the children help keep the house clean, and you will learn that being clean is very important to her. Once you learn how important being clean is to her, and you clean up for her periodically, you may notice that her response at night to your romantic advancements may be better than ever before.

Noticing what your wife watches on television and noticing the programs she enjoys the most can teach you things you need to do. I noticed my wife often watches home and garden shows. She is interested in home-improvement and home-beautification shows. Programs about wallpaper, flowers, crafts, designs, and anything to beautify the home always captured her attention. Having noticed her love of watching homes being decorated and beautified, I told her that if she does the designing and choosing of the material, I will do the work of putting up the wallpaper, painting the wall trim, and installing the floor tile.

Once my wife and I began working on the house together, we had great fun; we communicated more, and were drawn closer together. The trips to the different home-improvement stores, the paint stores, and the wallpaper stores, were adventures that united us together under a common cause. Noticing what she was doing when she had not said anything to me, caused me to learn to do things she loved.

8. Trial and error does work

Not only does noticing what she does when she doesn't say anything help you to learn about your wife, but trial and error also helps you to learn. You will just have to try different things, and then notice her response to them. This will take (1) much imagination and guesswork, (2) much energy and effort, and (3) constantly working at it. Always think of new and exciting things to try with your wife. Go places where you have not been before, and do not be afraid to go to the same places twice. Try new restaurants, new clothing styles, and new hairdos. Life should be an adventure for you and your spouse. Take away the adventure, and you will end up with a boring marriage and possible contentions between you and her.

Some wives will never make suggestions on what to do and where to go. She does not make those suggestions because she expects her husband to always do it. She feels that he is the man; and it is his duty to suggest going out to dinner, taking weekend trips, and whatever activities the family is supposed to do together. You can always ask your wife what she would like to do, but when she does not tell you, then it is up to you to come up with things to do.

Do not take her "none suggestions" as an indication of her not wanting to do anything at all; take it as in indication that it is time for you use to your imagination in the area of family-activity planning. Failing to plan activities for your family can lead to a boring family life and may cause your family to go in separate directions when seeking fun things to do. Husbands, keep your family united in fun by constantly coming up with fun things you and your family can do together. Always pray asking God the Father in Jesus' name to reveal fun, different, and unique activities for you and your family to do.

When seeking to dwell with your wife according to the knowledge you have learned about her, you must learn to observe your wife's negative reactions to certain things you do. She may never openly complain, but by her reaction to you, you should know whether she likes something or not. Husbands, we are so busy doing what we want that we sometimes fail to notice how our wives really feel. We must learn to be sensitive to our wives, and when we realize we are doing something they do not like, we must change what we are doing.

9. Verbal communication

Verbal communication is also a major part of getting to know your wife. There should be times when you and she get away just to talk. Take her out to dinner, take her for long walks, or take her into your bedroom where you and she can be alone—not for sex nor for sleeping but for talking. When talking to your wife, don't forget to listen. Let her talk to you, and give her the right to say what she feels without you getting upset. Allow her to be open and honest with you as you seek to listen with a caring and understanding heart. Remember what she says, and then make the proper changes in your life and marriage. Nonverbal communication is also a good way to get to know your wife. Holding her, being in her presence, and caressing her are acts of nonverbal communication that draws you and her closer together.

10. Romance, understanding, and tender loving care

When seeking to dwell with your wife according to the knowledge you have learned (and are learning) about her, don't forget to do those things that are normal to women. Most women love roses, candy, and cards. They enjoy romantic evenings and special moments. Holidays, birthdays, and anniversaries are all special to her, and it really hurts her when you forget, or if you remember but fail to do something special for her. Women are creatures of emotions. Allow her to cry at times; and give her the security of your strong, warm, loving, and caring embraces. She needs those at times.

A wife needs to know that her husband loves her, and to him, she is the most important person in the world. She needs to know that her husband thinks she is very attractive to him, and that she has a personality that pleases him. There are times when she needs to be held by him when no sex or romance is expected. Special gifts, sweet comments about her, and other gestures of love should be a constant part of what her husband does for her. These things are not to be done for special occasions only, but they are to be done "just because."

11. Your wife is intelligent

Another thing husbands need to learn about their wives is that they are intelligent people with the capacity to make decisions on their own. Allow her to make certain decisions without having to ask you first. If she makes a mistake, don't get upset; just remember all of the mistakes you made when making decisions, and then give her credit for being human. Always value her opinion, and frequently ask for her suggestions. On all major decisions that affect the entire family, she is to consult with you; however, on other decisions she may be confronted with, give her the freedom to decide as she thinks best.

12. Give her some space at times

Women need space and time alone. The stress of work, home, children, husband, and the other things she has to deal with can be overwhelming at times. There will be times when she will need to get away from all of that and get to herself. Allow her to have her quiet time of self-pampering and quiet meditation. Allow her to be able to do things for herself and to do things that do not include her family. To allow her to have private space and time for herself is not always easy for a man to do. We want them so involved in our world, and we in theirs, that it is hard for us to let go. If you value the sanity of your wife and if you don't want her to become an emotional wreck, you must give her that quiet time.

It is God's will for husbands to please their wives. God knew that in order for you to please her, you must know what He says about women and wives. He also knew that you must also know your wife. If you are a Christian husband, you are responsible for making your marriage the best it can be. God, in His Word, has given you the instructions you need in order to accomplish that task. Part of God's instructions to husbands is to dwell with your wife according to the knowledge He gives, and according to the knowledge of things you have learned about her.

Father; never allow me to underestimate, nor take for granted, the awesome, amazing, and outstanding attributes You have infused in my wife. Help me to tap into the intelligence, the intuition, and spiritual discernment You have placed in her. She truly is a prized and valuable possession that You have entrusted into my care. Please help all husbands to recognize the intelligence and value of their wives. In Jesus' name I pray; amen.

Jesus my LORD; You knew who I would need in order to fulfill Your Divine call on my life. Thank You for leading me to her; and thank You for placing her into my life. I trust You to develop me into the kind of husband and man she can love with all her heart, and be proud of. May You forever be glorified through this marriage.

Jesus is LORD

CHAPTER 12

Giving Honor to Your Wife

1. What giving honor to your wife means.

2. Why you should give honor to your wife.

3. What does being the weaker vessel mean?

4. Although the woman is called the weaker vessel; she deserves more honor and glory than the man.

5. Giving your wife honor as the weaker vessel:
   A. You give honor to your wife as the weaker vessel by loving her.
   B. You give honor to your wife as the weaker vessel by treating her the best you can.
   C. You give honor to your wife as the weaker vessel by protecting her.
   D. You give honor to your wife as the weaker vessel by supporting and encouraging her.
   E. You give honor to your wife as the weaker vessel by being a honorable person yourself.

God's Divine Instructions To Husbands and Men

1. What giving honor to your wife means

While God tells wives to reverence their husbands, [33] *"Nevertheless let every one of you in particular so love his wife even as himself; and the wife see that she reverence her husband (Ephesians.5:33),"* He tells husbands to give honor to their wives. [7] *Giving honour unto the wife, as unto the weaker vessel. (1st Peter. 3:7)*

To give honor means to give the highest respect to; to recognize as special and valuable; and to hold in high esteem. God knows that every wife needs to feel that her husband honors her, and respects her with the greatest amount of honor and respect he can give to her. God also knows that every wife needs to know that her husband thinks she is special and of great value to him. That is why He tells husbands honor their wives.

Do you show your wife that you honor her to the highest? Do you always give her the greatest respect you can? Do you treat your wife in such ways that it shows you think she is special, and of supreme value to you? If you are not, you are disobeying God, you are treating your wife far lower than you should, and you are causing your marriage to be less than it should be.

2. Why you should give honor to your wife

Every husband should give honor to his wife because it is one of the wisest things he can do in their marriage. Honoring your wife increases the joy in your home, and will cause your wife to appreciate you more and love you more. Honoring your wife is also a command that God charges all husbands to perform. While God says you are to honor her, He did not say she had to earn that honor or deserve it. You do not honor your wife because she has done something to win your honor, you do not honor your wife because of what she possesses, nor do you honor your wife because of her beauty. You honor her for two major reasons:

1. Because she is your wife.
2. Because God tells you to.

Even when your wife does something you do not like, and something that may bring shame on you and your family, you are still to treat her in an honorable way. If she sins in such ways that you feel you should end the marriage, you are to still give her honor. There was a woman in the Bible whose husband thought she has committed a sin against him that was worthy of her being put to death. Instead of embarrassing her and causing her to be put to death, he wanted to do the honorable thing and put her away privately. He honored her so much that even when he thought she had done something wrong, he was willing to give her a secret divorce (Mattew.1:18-25).

This woman was Mary, the mother of Jesus. The man was Joseph, her husband. Mary had not committed any sin. Although Joseph thought she had, he was still willing to do the honorable thing for her.

When you give honor to your wife regardless of what she does, (1) it shows you love God enough to obey Him, (2) it shows you are a just and honorable man yourself, and (3) it shows that you do love your wife.

3. What does it mean to be the weaker vessel mean?

⁷ Giving honour unto the wife, as unto the weaker vessel. *(1ˢᵗ Peter. 3:7)*

To be the weaker vessel means that the wife, in the sight of God, holds a lower position of authority in the home. This does not mean the wife is inferior to her husband; it just means that although they are equal in quality and value, when it comes to rank and order in the home; God has given the man greater authority.

Many women are not comfortable with terms and phrases such as "weaker vessel," "submit yourself to your husband," and "obey your husband." These terms are not a put-down to women, nor does it mean that God has a negative view of women. It simply means that God knew that for a home and marriage to function properly, there has to be rank and order. Thus, God placed the woman in a position where her husband is the head of her.

23 For the husband is the head of the wife, even as Christ is the head of the church. (Ephesians.5:23)

3 But I would have you know, that the head of every man is Christ; and the head of the woman is the man; and the head of Christ is God. (1st Corinthians.11:3)

4. Although the woman is called the weaker vessel; she deserves more honor and glory than the man.

We as humans like to give honor to the strong and brave while giving dishonor to the weak and feeble. We want to honor the ones that are the most gifted in their field of endeavor. We usually hold no honors for those who we think are weak and are not out front where they can be seen. We only honor those who we feel have achieved some outstanding level of accomplishment. However, God does things differently from what the world does. God tells saints to take the weaker and give them more honor. God said to take the less honorable and give them more abundant honor.

23 And those members of the body, which we think to be less honourable, upon these we bestow more abundant honour; and our uncomely parts have more abundant comeliness. (1st Corinthians 12:23)

God calls her the weaker vessel so that the husband will give her more abundant honor than he receives from her. All husbands need to realize that if it was not for his wife, he would have no glory.

*7 For a man indeed ought not to cover his head, forasmuch as **<u>he is the image and glory of God: but the woman is the glory of the man.</u>** (1st Corinthians.11:7)*

Husbands are the glory of God; wives are the glory of their husbands. Because your wife is what brings glory to you, you should honor her with great honors. You should do all you can to help her dress in ways that will bring you glory. You should talk about her in ways that will bring you glory. You should help her to learn the Word of God and to obey it so she can bring you glory. While you are doing all of these and more, remember the greatest thing you can do to help your wife bring you glory is to give her honor as the weaker vessel, and to love her with all your heart.

5. Giving your wife honor as the weaker vessel

*⁷ **Giving honour unto the wife**, as unto the weaker vessel. (1ˢᵗ Peter. 3:7)*

*A. You give honor to your wife as the
weaker vessel by loving her.*

It is a dishonor to a wife to have a husband who does not love her. It is a dishonor to a wife to have a husband who loves her but does not show his love for her consistently, regularly, and openly in public. The love that brings honor to a wife and glory to a husband, is a love that is told and a love that is shown. It is shown to her, and it is shown to others. Everyone should be able to tell by your actions and words that you truly love your wife with all of your heart.

Are you constantly doing things to show your wife that you love her? What are some of the things you have done lately to show your love for her? Going to work, having a place to stay, and paying all of the bills are not an adequate show of love. You would do those things even if you did not have a wife. Things like that are more of a show of courtesy than anything else. These things are also the commonplace things. A show of true love not only includes the common things you do, but it also includes the special things you do just for her and for her alone.

Not only is the love that brings honor to a wife and glory to a husband a love that is shown, it is also a love that is expressed in spoken words and in gestures of affection. You should always tell your wife you love her, and you should always tell her <u>why</u> you love her. Daily, tell her wonderful things about herself, and do not forget to also show special gestures of love that will say to her that you love her. Holding her, caressing her, and pampering her are unspoken gestures that show your love.

B. You give honor to your wife as the weaker vessel by treating her the best you can.

Many husbands can say they treat their wife well, but few can say they treat their wife the best they can. If you are a husband who would have to admit that you can treat your wife a little better than you have been treating her, you are a husband who is admitting that you are not properly honoring your wife, and thus you are disobeying the command of God to honor your wife as the weaker vessel. Start today treating your wife the best you can. Start today learning how to treat her better so you will always improve in the way you treat her. Always improving in the way you treat your wife, will cause you to always improve in the way you honor her.

C. You give honor to your wife as the weaker vessel by protecting her.

A wife who cannot find security in her husband is a wife who feels her husband is not honoring her. You are to always do your best to protect your wife from physical harm. She is to know that if anyone tries to hurt her, you will do all you can to protect her. She also needs to feel your protection for her against the stresses and the problems of life. Bill collectors, high-pressure salesmen, and disrespecting visitors are never to harass your wife. She should know you will not allow anyone to disrespect her, or harass her. She should know that you are her knight in shining armor who is always available, and who is always willing to protect her.

D. You give honor to your wife as the weaker vessel by supporting and encouraging her.

There are many things in life that your wife will need your support and encouragement in. She needs to know you are with her in the things she does in life. Let her know you are there to help uphold her, and you have great confidence in her ability to strive to accomplish the things she desires to accomplish. You should encourage her as a wife, mother, homemaker, career person, and woman. Encourage her as your best friend, as the one who helps to make you the best person you can be, and as the one who helps make your life and home the best it could ever be.

> *E. You give honor to your wife as the weaker vessel by being a honorable person yourself.*

²³ **<u>Her husband is known in the gates,</u>** when he sitteth among the elders of the land. (Proverbs.31:23)

You bring honor to your wife when people say good things about you. Every husband who is known for foolishness, wickedness, and for possessing a bad reputation, dishonors his God, himself, his wife, and his children. The best way, and the only way, to live an honorable life and be an honorable person is to live in obedience to the Word of God. Always increase in the knowledge of the Word of God, and in obedience to the Word of God, and you will always increase in being an honorable person.

Father; from a total disgrace to being covered with Your amazing grace. Father; I could never say thank You enough. Your grace has not only saved my soul through Jesus Christ; but it has also transformed me into a husband You are well pleased with. Because of Your grace, I strive by the power of the Holy Ghost to act in honorable, decent, and upright ways. I strive to live in ways that pleases my wife, my children, and myself. Thank You for developing me into an honorable husband and man.

Jesus my LORD; because I represent You in my home and marriage, I must increase in being honorable, decent, and upright. Because You are the perfect picture of honorable; I must strive to be a reflection of that picture. I truly want to be like You in my marriage, and in every area of my life.

Jesus is LORD

CHAPTER 13

Heirs Together of the Grace of Life

1. The husband is to realize that he and his wife are heirs together of the grace of life.

2. The hindrance of sin.

3. Overcoming the hindrance of sin.

4. How divorce affects the grace of life for a husband and wife.

5. Valuing your wife's opinion and suggestions.

6. The grace of life
   A. The grace of life includes the fact that you have life.
   B. The grace of life deals more with inward blessings and its effect on every area of your life than it does with outward possessions.
   C. If you are involved in something and it does not somehow allow you to bring glory to God through it and in it, it is not a part of the grace of life that God has for you.
   D. The grace of life also includes loving and being loved.

7. Hindered Prayers.

God's Divine Instructions To Husbands and Men

1. The husband is to realize that he and his wife are heirs together of the grace of life

⁷ And as being heirs together of the grace of life. (1ˢᵗ Peter. 3:7)

The grace of life. God has great plans for your life. There are certain things He wants you to accomplish in life, and certain blessings He wants to give you. He wants your life to be filled with joy, and to be fulfilling in every area. All of these things (and more) will only be experienced and enjoyed by you as a result of you being married to your wife. You and she are heirs together of the grace of life. All of the grace and blessings God has for you in this life are not just for you alone; it is for you and her together. Without her, you do not get the best God has to offer you in this life.

The greatest plans God has for your life includes your wife. The greatest joys God has for you to experience include the joys that He will give you because she is a part of your heart and life. The greatest blessings (other than Christ) you will receive, you will receive as a joint blessing for you and her together. When God mapped out the best course for your life, He mapped out a course you can only walk when you and she walk it together. When you (after you have married her) walk on a course without her, (and it is your fault she is no longer with you); you are walking down a course of life that is less than God's best for you. When you try (after you have married her) to walk a course with someone else, (and it's your fault you and your wife are no longer together), you are walking down a course that is less than God's best for you.

Being heirs together. To be an heir means to be a recipient of something someone else gives to you that you did not have to work for nor earn. They did what was necessary to provide the things they wanted to give to you. They also are the ones to set the guidelines on what you must do in order to receive the inheritance they want to give you. If you fulfill their guidelines, you will, at the proper time, receive the inheritance. One of the guidelines God gives in order for you to receive many of the inherited blessings He has for you, is for you to be married to your wife, and for you to treat her as He has instructed in His Word. If you are not treating your wife as God has instructed, and because of your faults you and her are no longer together, you are missing out on many of the inherited blessings God has for you.

¹³And this have ye done again, covering the altar of the LORD with tears, with weeping, and with crying out, insomuch that he regardeth not the offering any more, or receiveth it with good will at your hand. ¹⁴Yet ye say, Wherefore? Because the LORD hath been witness between thee and the wife of thy youth, against whom thou hast dealt treacherously: yet is she thy companion, and the wife of thy covenant. (Malachi.2:13-14)

2. The hindrance of sin

When there is sin in your life, it causes God to withdraw His hand of blessing from you and from your life. Sin has the potential of preventing you from receiving many of the blessings God has for you. When you know to treat your wife right but you don't do it, it is sin, and it is causing you to miss out on many of God's blessings for you and your life.

¹ Behold, the LORD'S hand is not shortened, that it cannot save; neither his ear heavy, that it cannot hear: ² But your iniquities have separated between you and your God, and your sins have hid his face from you, that he will not hear. (Isaiah.59:1-2)

Are you wondering why things seem to be going wrong in your life? Are you wondering why you do not seem to be prospering? You try hard, you work hard, you have great ideas, but nothing seems to be working for you. If you want your life to turn around for the better, start treating your wife as God has instructed.

¹⁶ Wash you, make you clean; put away the evil of your doings from before mine eyes; cease to do evil; ¹⁷ Learn to do well; seek judgment, relieve the oppressed, judge the fatherless, plead for the widow. ¹⁸ Come now, and let us reason together, saith the LORD: though your sins be as scarlet, they shall be as white as snow; though they be red like crimson, they shall be as wool. ¹⁹ If ye be willing and obedient, ye shall eat the good of the land: (Isaiah.1:16-19)

Just as a husband can hinder the blessings of God in his life and in the life of his family, so can the wife hinder the blessings of God for them as well. If she has sin in her life and/or if she is not treating her husband as God instructs in His Word, it can cause the husband and family to miss many of the blessings that God has for them. Her sins and/or mistreatment of her husband can disrupt the peace and harmony of a home, cause problems and difficulties in the home, and make the marriage and home less than what God intended for it to be. When Eve yielded to the temptation of the devil and also convinced her husband to yield, (1) it destroyed their fellowship with God, (2) it caused shame to come upon them, (3) it caused them to be cursed, (4) it caused them to be kicked out of the most beautiful place on earth, and (5) it brought sin into their life and upon the human race. (See, Genesis.3)

3. Overcoming the hindrance of sin

While a husband cannot always prevent a wife from sinning, there are certain things he can do to help safeguard her and the family. First, he is to become a Christian himself, and then he is to seek the salvation of his wife and family. They are to be growing in the grace and knowledge of God, and they are to be growing in their obedience to the written Word of God. The more a person becomes dedicated and devoted to God, the less likely they will become engulfed in sinful behavior.

Next, the husband is to treat his wife according to God's instructions for a husband as found in the Holy Bible. A wife who has a husband who obeys what God says, is a wife who is less likely to sin against her husband. Also, the husband is to constantly pray with his wife and family. Together, they are to pray, asking God to keep them from temptations and sin, and to cause them to always live in a way where they can continually receive the wonderful blessings God has for them.

When a wife is involved in sin, it will affect the family in negative ways. Husbands, it is your responsibility to talk to your wife about her sins, and then work with her to cause her to repent. Do not become involved in sin yourself; but through prayer, patience, love, and obedience to the Word of

God, fight against satan, sin, and unrighteousness. The blessings of God can be restored in the home if you remain faithful to God, and if your wife repents. If you remain faithful and she does not repent, God will bless you to the fullest that He can, and He will chasten her in such ways that it will cause her to yield the peaceable fruits of righteousness.

4. How divorce affects the grace of life for a husband and wife

Being heirs together of the grace of life ties you and her together that what affects one affects both. Both are blessed, and both must endure misfortunes together. God no longer sees each as distinct individuals, but He views you and her as one. Your life and her life are so tied together that whatever blessings you and she receive, you and she receive them as joint heirs together.

When a marriage ends in divorce for a non-biblical reason and the couple goes their separate ways, they often separate, thinking the worst is now behind them and the best is ahead of them. What they fail to realize is that the best they could have had was to treat each other as God has said and thus receive God's blessings. Your ways are not better than God's ways nor are your ways as good as God's ways; thus, if you and your spouse divorce because you were not treating her right, you have forever missed out on your best days. If the divorce is not your fault because you did your best in the marriage, God can bless you with better days ahead.

If you are divorced and remarried and the divorce was your fault, confess and repent of all sins, and then begin treating your present wife as God instructed; God will then begin to bless this marriage to be the best it can be. Confession and repentance are powerful tools that will cause the blessings of God to flow in your life again. You may have missed out on certain blessings because of sin, but you have not missed out on all of your blessings. God loves to forgive, and He loves to start blessing you from where you are now. We serve a great God who is so wonderful and so merciful. He is slow to anger and quick to mercy. He is a God of grace and restoration. He will grant unto you His grace, and He will restore rivers of blessings unto you.

Knowing that you and your wife are heirs together should cause you to realize how important your wife is to you. She holds the key to many of God's wonderful blessings for you. You should treat her extra special because the better you treat her, the better your blessings will be. You should do all you can to hold on to her because to hold on to her is to hold on to your blessings. Always remember that in the sight of God when you find a wife, you find a good thing and obtain favor of the Lord.

[22] *Whoso findeth a wife findeth a good thing, and obtaineth favour of the LORD. (Proverbs.18:22)*

When you lose a wife (because you did not treat her as God instructed), you lose a good thing, and you miss out on the favor (the great blessings God had for you because you were married to her) of the Lord. What are you missing out on because you are not treating your wife as God says? Repent today so that today you can return to the path that leads to God's great and awesome blessings for you, for your wife, and for your children.

5. Valuing your wife's opinion and suggestions

Being heirs together should also cause you to include your wife's opinion and input in every major decision you make in life. You are not making decisions just for yourself; the decisions you make are for you and her together. What you do affects her, and what she does affects you. Because the decisions will affect both, both should be in on the decision-making process. View her as an intelligent person and one capable of adding valuable input into your decision-making process. Realize God has given her "a woman's intuition," and although she may not be able to tell you why something should or should not be done, she will know in her heart if something is the right thing to do or not.

Husbands, don't be afraid to alter the course of your life if your wife doesn't agree with the things you are doing or the things you are about to do. If you and she cannot come to an agreement on a thing, then the thing may need to be changed. The only time you can go against what your wife says is if you are convinced within your heart that to obey your wife is to disobey God. God will confirm whether or not you are right or wrong.

¹⁵ Let us therefore, as many as be perfect, be thus minded: **_and if in any thing ye be otherwise minded, God shall reveal even this unto you._** *(Philippians.3:15)*

It is very important for you to be able to discern what the will of God is, and what is not in the will of God. If something is in violation of God's written Word, it is not the will of God for you. If you are about to make a decision and the peace of God does not come upon your heart (or if your conscience bothers you), it may not be the will of God for you. Much prayer, meditation, and spiritual counseling should be done whenever there is a disagreement between you and your wife over a decision you are about to make.

6. The Grace of Life

The grace of life is a term that refers to all of the unearned blessings God wants to give you. This does not refer to the blessing of salvation by grace through faith in Jesus Christ. You can receive this blessing of grace without your spouse, and it is not hinged on you having a spouse. Once you get married, all the blessings you will receive from God (other than salvation) will be for you and your wife's benefit together.

*A. The grace of life includes
the fact that you have life.*

You did nothing to earn being born; it is because of God's grace you have life. God did not give you life just for your own benefit; He gave you life so you could spend part of it with your wife. It was God's plan for your wife to be happy and fulfilled; thus, God gave you life so you could be part of what He uses to bring happiness and fulfillment to her life. How well are you doing at fulfilling the call of God to be part of what He is using to try to bring happiness and fulfillment to your wife? Does your wife thank God for you, or does she regret being married to you? Is God happy that He gave you life because you are using that life to fulfill His will in loving your wife like Christ loves the church?

Every husband should possess the attitude that the fact that they have life is more for their wife's benefit than it is for himself. When you become a Christian, your life no longer belongs to you; it belongs to God. When you become a husband, your life no longer belongs to you; it belongs to God and to your wife. Your three major goals should be (1) to please God, (2) to please your wife, and (3) to please your family. This does not exclude doing good things to and for others, because if you are doing things to please God, you will be doing things that will be a blessing and help to others.

B. The grace of life deals more with inward blessings and its effect on every area of your life than it does with outward possessions.

God blesses you with outward physical possessions, but the joy you get from them is never to be greater than the inward joy and peace that comes from Jesus Christ. Many marriages break up over physical possessions more than they break up over anything else. We have put more value on the pleasures that things bring, than we have on the pleasures our spouse and our God can bring to us. We argue over money, possessions, and things. We neglect one another in pursuit of money, possessions, and things. Once we get the money, possessions, and things, we soon realize that money, possession, and things do not totally satisfy.

We as men think that physical possessions are of great worth; and we are only successful and prosperous when we have many physical possessions. There are some families, however, who wish that the father and husband would sell or give away most of their physical possessions, stop trying to get more, and then spend his greatest energy trying to build a relationship with them. God's view of physical possessions and physical riches are totally different from ours.

God says physical possessions can cause a person to be wretched, miserable, poor, blind, and naked in His eyes (Revelation.3:15-18). God says they can cause a person to fall into the temptations and snares of the devil, and they can fall into many foolish and hurtful lusts that can draw them into destruction and perdition. The love of money (gain) is the root of all evil (1st

Timothy.6:9-10). To have an overabundance of riches can also be a witness against you (James.5:1-3).

It is not to be thought that riches in themselves are evil; it is what men allow riches to do to them that is evil. It is possible to be rich and to be godly. When a man is rich and godly, he knows how to use his riches in a way that will glorify God, and he knows how to put the proper value on his riches. He will never let his riches keep him from the most important things of life. Those things are his God, his family, and his proper relationships with others.

While physical riches may be included as part of the grace of life, one is to never measure the grace of life by the physical riches they have or do not have. The grace of life, first of all, includes peace within one's heart. Jesus has given us His peace, and if something steals your inner peace, it may not be a thing that God is including as part of the grace of life for you. If there is something that is part of the grace of life for you and it does not bring peace, it is because you are not using it properly, nor are you obeying God concerning it.

C. If you are involved in something and it does not somehow allow you to bring glory to God through it and in it, it is not a part of the grace of life that God has for you.

Peace, contentment, and bringing glory to God are all gauges to determine the grace of life for you. In all that you do, you are to do to the glory of God. If you can't ultimately glorify God because of what you are doing, you should not be doing it. The grace of life that God grants to you will bring glory to his name. When you treat your spouse as God says, people will see how great of a husband you are, and will give glory to God. Bringing glory to God is always a grace that will enrich and fulfill your life.

D. The grace of life also includes loving and being loved.

While there are many different types of love, the greatest earthly love that you should give to another human being is the love you give to your wife. The greatest earthly love that you should receive from another human being is the love you receive from your wife. While loving others and being loved by others are important and necessary, your grace of life includes that very special love that you are to give to your wife, and that very special love that you are to receive from your wife.

If you are not giving your greatest love to your wife, you are missing out on a very important part of the grace of life that God has for you. Giving love is the greatest thing you can do because when you give love, it prompts you to always give your best, and do your best. God so loved that he gave his best. He gave his son Jesus Christ. Jesus so loved that he gave his best. His best was redeeming men by sacrificing His life. Giving love is always much better than receiving it. The greatest earthly love you will ever experience in this life is not the love you receive from others, nor the love you receive from your wife. The greatest earthly love that you will experience in this life is the Christ kind of love that you give to your wife.

Giving love is always greater than receiving it. The love God gives is much greater than the love He receives from those whom He gives His love to. You will never love God as much as He loves you. God's greatest joy comes from giving love, and not just from receiving love only. He enjoys giving love to sinners, but He does not enjoy receiving the love they give back to Him, because they do not give love back to Him. God enjoys giving us His perfect love, but we do not always give Him perfect love in return. God enjoys our love, but He enjoys more the love He gives us.

It is not how much your spouse loves you that matters the most; it is how much you love your spouse that matters the most. If you are not giving the fullness of your love to your wife, you are not being like God, and you are missing out on the grace of life in the area of love. Never make the tragic mistake of forming an attitude that says, "If she does not love me, I will not love her. If she does not show love to me, I will not show love to her." Regardless of her response to you and to your love, you are to always give her your greatest love. She may reject it, she may not respond to it, or she may receive only a small portion of it; but regardless of what she does, you are to keep giving her the greatest love you can give her.

Giving her your greatest love may hurt at times; but you will always feel better when you realize that you have loved her to the fullest. A man can look at his dying wife and hurt greatly, but he can find sweet relief in knowing he loved her to the fullest while he could. Even after a divorce, a man finds great comfort in knowing that he has tried his best and has given his greatest love even though the marriage did not succeed. Great is the pain, and great is the torment of a man who looks at his dying wife (or divorced wife) and realizes that he did not do his best, nor did he love her with all of his heart.

My heart always goes out to the man who refuses to love his wife to the fullest that he can. I feel for him because I know he is refusing the greatest thing he could ever do in this life. If he becomes great in every area of life except in the area of loving his wife, he really has become nothing (1st Corinthians. 13:1-3) (the word *charity* in this passage of scripture can be translated into the word *love*). Because he refuses to love his wife fully, he will never know true contentment in life, he will never experience the true joys of life, he will never know the true successes of life, and he will never know true fulfillment in life.

No area in a man's life will ever be totally perfect if he fails in the area of loving his wife to the fullest. He will never be totally satisfied with anything, regardless of how well his life seems to be, if he does not fully love his wife. God has so tied the grace of life for you with your love for your wife that if you fail in the area of love, you fail in receiving the total grace of life God has for you.

7. Hindered Prayers

⁷ Likewise, ye husbands, dwell with them according to knowledge, giving honour unto the wife, as unto the weaker vessel, and as being heirs together of the grace of life; <u>**that your prayers be not hindered.**</u> *(1ˢᵗ Peter. 3:7)*

To be able to receive answers to prayers should be one of the most important things to a Christian husband and father. Prayer will get you your greatest job, prayer will bring protection on you and your family, and prayer will keep your children off drugs and out of sin. Prayer will also help to make your marriage the best it can be.

There are five major things that will hinder and stop a husband's prayers from being answered: (1) not praying at all, (2) not continuously confessing and repenting of sin, (3) not forgiving others, (4) not praying in faith, and (5) not dwelling with your wife according to knowledge, not giving her honor as the weaker vessel, and not honoring her as an heir with you of the grace of life.

The first four of these hindrances to prayer deals with your relationship to God and others, while the fifth deals with your relationship with your wife. When your relationship with your wife is not right, your relationship with God will be affected. God so values your relationship with your wife, that He may not answer your prayers if you are not obeying His instructions on how to treat your wife.

There is nothing this life has to offer equal to the blessings of treating your wife right. Treating her right causes you to have favor with God, and it also causes God to hear and answer your prayers. What is greater than favor with God and Him answering your prayers? When you treat your wife as God instructs, God will bless you and all that pertains to you. There will be times of hardships and difficulties, yet you will experience the presence of God and the deliverance of God. Husbands, be sure that in all things, you are treating your wife as God instructed, because to not do so will cause you to miss out on many of the best blessings that you could ever receive, even the blessing of getting prayers answered.

There are things money cannot buy and men cannot fix. There are problems that seem to have no answers, and situations you just cannot handle. When confronted with those things, and with other problems and situations, it is comforting to know that you have a God that hears and answers prayer. It is even more comforting to know that God will hear and answer your prayers because you have been treating your wife as He instructed. You need your prayers for yourself answered, your family needs your prayers for them answered, and others need your prayers for them answered. Treat your wife as God instructed for your sake, your family's sake, and for others' sake.

Jesus is LORD

CHAPTER 14

Receiving the Right Wife

1. The two greatest decisions a man must make.

2. Make sure you are the right kind of man God would want one of His daughters to marry.

3. Do not seek a wife; seek God, and let Him bring the right woman to you, or you to her.

4. Do not consider an unsaved woman to marry.

5. Do not consider marrying a saved woman who is not seeking to live holy, and is not dedicated to God.

6. Seek to marry God's choice even if God chooses someone you would not choose for yourself (Hosea 3:1-3).

7. When contemplating marriage, learn the qualities of a virtuous woman (Proverbs.1:10-31), and then only consider marrying such a woman.

God's Divine Instructions To Husbands and Men

1. The two greatest decisions a man must make

While you as a man are constantly confronted with many decisions, there are two decisions that will be the most important decisions you will ever make. The first is your decision about salvation, and the second is your decision about marriage. When you make the right decision about salvation (the right decision is to accept Jesus Christ as your Lord and Savior), (1) you will spend eternity with Jesus Christ, (2) you will be under the blessings of God, (3) you will have God's help in every area of life, and (4) you will have available to you all of the promises God has made to His children.

When you make the wrong decision about salvation (the wrong decision is to reject Jesus Christ as your Lord and Savior), (1) you will spend eternity in the lake of fire, (2) you will remain under the curse of the law and not under the blessings of God, (3) you will not receive the fullness of God's help in your life even though He will bless you and help you in certain areas, and (4) you cannot claim any of the promises God makes to those who love Him and are His children.

The decision you make about whom to marry (if you decide to marry) will carry a lifetime of consequences that can be good, bad, or both. Marrying the right woman (if you are the right type of man) can lead to a life of fulfillment, victory over difficulties, and a life of having someone there who will love you, and be there for you all the days of her life. It can lead to having a wonderful family and a great life.

To make the wrong decision about whom to marry can lead to discontentment, hardships, and a possible divorce. It can lead to your children being hurt by the devastation of divorce, or it could lead to them living in a dysfunctional home. It can also lead to abuse, adultery, abandonment, and other destructive behaviors by one or both spouses. To make the wrong decision can lead to a lifetime of misery and regret.

There are certain things every man who is contemplating marriage should consider. Many men usually make their decision of whom to marry based on (1) how good the woman looks, (2) how she makes him feel emotionally, and (3) and how much fun they have together. These are not very good criteria to base marriage on because (1) looks can change, (2) emotions can decrease and even diminish, and (3) there will be times in every marriage where fun will be replaced by difficulties. If you are going to make the right decision about whom to marry, you may need to base your decision on the following points.

2. Make sure you are the right kind of man God would want one of His daughters to marry

Before you start desiring the right type of woman to marry, make sure you are the right type of man God would want one of His daughters to marry. The right type of man is a saved man who is doing his best to live according to the Word of God. God is not going to send one of His daughters to marry you if you are not a Christian (2nd Corinthians. 6:14-18). God says Christians and sinners are never to marry each other. If you are not a Christian, your first desire should be to get saved before you start desiring to get a wife.

After becoming saved by accepting Jesus Christ as the Lord of your life, you must be seeking to live according to the Word of God as best you can. A man who is not interested in being all God tells him to be, will never be the type of man a woman would want him to be. The better Christian you are; the better husband you will be. A man who will not be faithful to his God (by keeping God's Word) will not be faithful to his wife. The more you grow in the things of God, the more you will learn what makes a good husband, and the more you will be able to become that good husband.

You do not have to wait until you are perfect before asking God for a wife; just make sure you are living the best you can. Although you are not without faults and you need much improvement, when God sees that you are constantly growing and improving, He may consider you to be ready for marriage. Show to God that you are the right type of person because (1) you are saved, (2) you are obeying the things you've learned from His Word, and (3) you are always seeking to learn more so you can do more. After God sees those things in you, He may consider you as a good candidate to marry one of His daughters.

3. Do not seek a wife; seek God, and let Him bring the right woman to you, or you to her

God is more interested in you having the right wife than you are. God knows who the right woman is for you, and He knows where she is. If you trust Him and acknowledge him in all your ways, He will direct your path to her (Proverbs.3:5-6). When the time is right and God determines that you are ready for a wife, He will cause you and that woman to come together, and He will reveal to you that she is the right one for you. When you seek a wife without God's help, you are responsible for finding her, and you will not know what you are getting. When you seek God, He will be responsible for sending you the right wife, and He knows what you will be getting.

God put Adam to sleep, took a rib from his side, and made a wife for him. When the woman was ready for him (and he was ready for the woman), God brought the woman to Adam (Genesis.2:20-25). Adam did not go seeking a wife; he just trusted God. Because he trusted God, God made the perfect woman for him, and brought her to him. God is in the process of perfecting a woman for you, and developing her into what He wants her to be. While he is preparing her, he is also in the process of perfecting you. When you are right, when she is right, and when the time is right, God will bring you two together.

God will also let you know that she is the right one for you. You will not wonder about it nor will you doubt it; you will know she is the one God has for you. Not only will you know she is right for you; she will know you are the one God has for her. God will reveal it to you and to her. Both of you will know you are right for each other.

Someone once said, "When in doubt, do without." If you have serious doubts about the woman you are about to marry, you may need to do without until you are sure. You are to be sure in your head but more so in your heart. When God brings the right woman to you, you will know deep within your heart she is the one. Your heart will be filled with peace, joy, and the assurance of knowing she is the one for you. You may be a little apprehensive and somewhat afraid, but you will know in your heart that she is the right one for you.

When seeking God for the right spouse, you are to date, you are to make friends, and you are to do none-sinful things with those of the opposite sex. You can have fun, fellowship, and friendship with women; but you are never to make a commitment until you know God has said to you, "This is the right one for you." You are to look your best and be your best. God will send her to you, but you must do your part in looking as attractive as you can, and developing an attractive personality.

If you love God and trust Him, you do not have to worry about marrying the wrong person because God promised that if you are about to do something that's against His will, He will reveal it unto you.

*^{14} I press toward the mark for the prize of the high calling of God in Christ Jesus. ^{15} Let us therefore, as many as be perfect, be thus minded: **and if in any thing ye be otherwise minded, God shall reveal even this unto you.*** (Philippians.3:14-15)

God promises that when you have a mind of only wanting to do His will and accept His choice, if you are about to do something outside His will, He will somehow and some way reveal to you that you are about to do the wrong thing. However, once He reveals it to you, you must make the difficult decision to change your actions. It will not be easy, and it will hurt and anger some people; however, it is better to change now than to live your life with the wrong person.

4. Do not consider an unsaved woman to marry

One of the major ways you can tell that a woman is not sent by God is if she is unsaved. When the devil sees that you desire to be married, he tries to send you one of his daughters to marry. He does this to keep you from marrying

God's choice for you. Regardless of how wonderful she seems to be and how right you and she seem for each other, if she is not saved, you are not to marry her. If she wants to marry you, she must first become a Christian, and the proof of her salvation must be evident in her life.

Don't start thinking that you can marry an unsaved woman, and she will eventually become a Christian. When a Christian marries a sinner, the sinner usually does not become godlier; usually, the Christian becomes more sinful. Never violate the Word of God by thinking you have a better way. If God says do not marry a sinner, then do not marry one. The number one principle in knowing the wrong woman to marry is if she is an unsaved person. The number one mistake a Christian man can make is to marry a sinner, hoping she will later become a Christian.

While there is an exception to every rule, you are probably not the exception to the rule of a saint not marrying a sinner. God told Hosea to marry a woman who was a prostitute, but it was for a special purpose that He was seeking to fulfill. It was also a marriage where the wife was constantly unfaithful to her husband. She brought much shame and hurt to herself, to him and to their children. It was a negative thing God used to send a message to His people.

If you decide to marry a sinner and the marriage seems to turn out to be a good marriage, you can be assured of this fact: it is still a marriage that falls far short of what God had for you if you would have married a saint. If you marry a sinner, you will never reach the level of satisfaction, joy, contentment, and ecstasy that God would have given you if you had married a saint. The underlying lessons to be learned from Hosea marrying a sinner is God can use it for His purpose; it will most likely lead to much heartaches and shame, and it will never be called one of the best marriages in the world.

If you are already married to someone who is a sinner, you need not seek a divorce, but you should seek God in dealing with her about becoming saved. You are to live the Christian lifestyle before her and always hold her up to God in prayer. Strive to make the marriage the best it can be, and teach your children the Word of God. Through these things, God may deal with her about salvation, and He will help to make the marriage the best it can be.

5. Do not consider marrying a saved woman who is not seeking to live holy and is not dedicated to God

The level of dedication a woman has to God shows the level of dedication a woman will have to her husband. If she is not totally dedicated to God, she will not be totally dedicated to her husband. If she will not live like God wants her to live, she will not live like her husband wants her to live. Don't think she will do for you what she will not do for God. This does not mean a Christian woman has to be perfect and without any faults. It simply means she should have a lifestyle where people can tell she loves the Lord, she is trying to live the best she can for the Lord; and she is growing in her love, devotion, knowledge, and obedience to the Lord. She may stumble, but she repents of her sins and then seeks to go forward in the Lord.

6. Seek to marry God's choice even if God chooses someone you would not choose for yourself (Hosea 3:1-3)

We as men must realize that marriage is for God's purposes and not just for our pleasure. There are things God wants to accomplish through our marriages, and we must be willing to allow Him to accomplish them. We must start by being willing to marry God's choice even when He chooses someone whom we would not choose for ourselves. Hosea would have never chosen for himself a wife of whoredom, but when he realized that she was God's choice for him, he denied himself and obeyed God. Develop a desire for God's will to be done, and then accept only God's choice for you.

God knows what is best for you, and He also knows what purposes He wants to fulfill through you. You must remember that you do not belong to you. You belong to God; and your number one desire should be for God's will to be done in you, for you, and through you. Seek to marry whom God wants you to marry and not just the one whom you want (that is if the one you want is not God's choice for you). To choose God's choice, you must be able to discern who God's choice is for you. There are certain ways you can discern God's choice.

*A. To discern God's choice,
you must begin with prayer.*

Never take the importance of prayer lightly. Prayer is a powerful tool that can alter the course of your life. Prayer causes God to become involved in your life to cause His will to be done. Your daily prayer should be one of thanking God because you believe He is sending you His choice of a wife. You are to pray, thanking God that He is causing you to know whom His choice is for you. You, most likely, will not be able to marry His choice if you do not know whom His choice is; therefore, you must pray, and you must believe that He will bring you too together and reveal to you that she is His choice for you.

*B. To discern God's choice,
you must have faith and trust in God.*

When seeking to discern God's choice for you, you will just have to say, "Lord, I am trusting that you are so involved in my life that you will make sure I don't marry anyone but your choice for me." If you come to the point where you begin to believe you will never find a good woman or that all the good women are taken, that is an indication that you do not have faith in God's ability to preserve the right woman for you, and to get her to you together. If you are going to receive God's choice, you must trust God regardless of what things seem like.

*C. To discern God's choice, you must acknowledge God
in all your ways so He can direct your path.*

The only way to acknowledge God in all of your ways is, to obey Him in all of your ways. Through your obedience, God will be able to direct you to His choice. Through your obedience, He can cause you to do the things necessary to cause the woman to know you are God's choice for her.

Obedience to God is a key component in receiving God's choice. However, when you travel down a path of disobedience, you are traveling down a path of destruction where God is not leading, and a path that may lead you to the wrong woman to marry.

When being obedient to God, a saint may stumble and fall into sin at times. When you sin, it does not keep you from God's choice, if you repent of the sin and return to obeying God again. Sin is a hindrance that can be removed with confession and repentance. If there is no confession and repentance of the sins you are committing, those sins become a barrier that may block you from God's choice.

D. To discern God's choice, you must be willing to be patient and to wait on God.

Before God's choice shows up in your life, the devil will try to send someone who seems right for you, but she will not be God's choice. Don't marry the first person that comes along, unless you are sure she is the one God is sending. You will meet quite a few women, and many will seem to make a good choice for a wife. You are not to settle for that good choice; you are to wait for God to give you His perfect choice. God will reveal to you if you are about to make the wrong choice.

[15] *Let us therefore, as many as be perfect, be thus minded: and if in any thing ye be otherwise minded, God shall reveal even this unto you. (Philippians.3:15)*

To wait for God does not mean to sit by and do nothing. It means to continue to do what God instructs you to do (developing a godly personality, obeying Him, looking your best, having friends of the opposite sex [but not sinning with them], praying, trusting, and believing Him, etc.) while waiting for God to do what you can't do (bring the right woman to you and revealing to you she is the right one).

7. When contemplating marriage, learn the qualities of a virtuous woman (Proverbs. 31:10-31), and then only consider marrying such a woman

The first principle of a virtuous woman that you must consider is that she is hard to find.

<u>Who can find a virtuous woman?</u> (Proverbs.31:10)

She is not the average woman, and it will take some time to find her. When seeking this type of woman, do not go to nightclubs or dens of iniquity, because she is not there. She is not at the liquor stores nor is she in the dope houses. When seeking this type of woman, begin in the church. She will be a woman who goes to church, and who is a church worker. She loves her God, and she loves her Lord Jesus Christ. She also greatly delights in the things of God. A virtuous woman can only be found in the right place, and the right place begins with the church. Learn to look in the right places, and learn to look for the right things. It may take much work, time, and effort; but it is all worth it in the end.

While it will be God bringing you and her together, you are responsible for allowing God to lead you to the right place at the right time. If you are going to nightclubs, dope houses, gambling dens, and casinos, it is not God leading you; and thus, He cannot bring her to you or you to her. While we realize that "God often works in mysterious ways, with wonders to perform" and that it is not impossible for God to lead you to the right woman in such places, we do know that God usually does not work in such a fashion. Oftentimes, if you are in those places, God did not lead you there; you led yourself there. The most important thing about going any place at any time is to be sure it is by the leading of the Holy Spirit and not you leading yourself.

The second principle of a virtuous woman that you must consider is that her value is far above rubies.

<u>For her price is far above rubies.</u> (Proverbs.31:10)

To be far above rubies means that she is a woman far above the average woman in many aspects. Women can be classified into two groups. The first is a woman of glass; the second is a woman whose value is far above rubies. Glass is cheap while rubies are expensive. Glass is common; rubies are rare. You must learn how to compare these two types of women and then be willing to pay the high price of receiving a woman whose value is far above rubies.

A cheap woman of glass is one in which a man can convince to engage in sexual relationships with him constantly before marriage. A woman whose value is above rubies is determined to refuse sexual relationships until after marriage, and then with her husband only. If she commits that sin, she quickly repents and refuses to continue in such acts. Are you willing to pay the price of waiting until after marriage to have sex with a virtuous woman, or are you willing to pay the cheap price of having constant sex before marriage with a cheap woman of glass?

A cheap woman of glass is willing to compromise her convictions in Christ and enter into many sins. A woman whose value is above rubies will stand firm on her convictions in Christ, and will seek to turn down sinful temptations. If she yields and commits a sin, she quickly repents and once again begins living in obedience to Christ.

Everyone need to also understand that a woman of glass can eventually become a virtuous woman. She should become that virtuous woman before you marry her, or she should at least be trying to become one. If you are already married to a woman who you think is a woman of glass, (1) change the way you think of her, and start thinking of her as a virtuous woman under construction; (2) start doing what you can to help her become a virtuous woman; (3) pray for her daily, and if possible, pray with her daily; (4) be a virtuous man; and (5) always put God and the things of God first in your life and home. She may have started out as a woman of glass; but by the grace of God, by your prayers and supplications, and by the hard work of you and her together, she can become a virtuous woman whose price is far above rubies.

Father; if I get what I want; I will end up not wanting what I got. When I get what You want, I will want what I get. My choice or Your choice; I choose Your choice. I chose your choice, and now 43 years later, I am still rejoicing over Your choice. Thank You for keeping me from my choice; and leading me to Your choice. Please grant all those seeking a spouse the wisdom to know Your choice for them, and then choosing Your choice for them. In Jesus' name I pray; amen.

Jesus my LORD; You have a Divine purpose for marriage. That Devine purpose can be fulfilled only with Your choice. I chose Your choice so Your will, plan, and purpose can be fulfilled in my marriage. Thank You for leading me to Your choice

Jesus is LORD

CHAPTER 15

Things That a Husband Should Never Do (Part 1)

1. Do's and don'ts, right avenues and wrong avenues.

2. Never slap, hit, abuse, or do anything to your wife that brings pain and hurt.

3. Never cheat on your wife.

4. Never lie to your wife.

5. Never embarrass your wife in public or before others.

1. Do's and don'ts, right avenues and wrong avenues

Life is filled with do's and don'ts. It is filled with things you should do and things you should never do. Life is filled with avenues that every man should venture to travel, but there are other avenues of life a man should never seek to travel. When a man does what he should, and travels the avenues that are best, his life can be an enriching and fulfilling adventure that leads to salvation and success. When he does what he should never do, and travels avenues he should never travel, his life can be a hell on earth that leads to disaster, destruction, and eternity in the lake of fire.

Not only is life filled with do's and don'ts, and right avenues and wrong avenues, marriage is also filled with do's and don'ts, and right avenues and wrong avenues. There are certain things in marriage that every husband must do if his marriage is going to be an enriching and fulfilling marriage. There are also things that a husband should never do because to do them may cause the wreck and ruin of his marriage. Many marriages are in trouble today, or have gone through some hard times because some husbands did what they should not have done, and did not do what they should have done.

As a husband, you should seek to find out the things a husband should never do and then seek to avoid doing them at all cost. Avoiding those things may cause your wife's love for you to increase, they may cause her respect for you to increase, and it may cause her to obey you more. Doing things you should never do may cause your wife to stop loving you, to stop respecting you, and to stop obeying you. It will lead to problems and difficulties that you would normally not have to face.

I want to discuss some of the major things a husband should never do in his marriage. While there are many things he should never do, I only want to discuss a few of the major ones. Obeying the things we discuss will cause him to avoid potential problems that can destroy his marriage. Someone once said, "Warning comes before destruction." Because such is true, this section of the book should be the warning that alerts men when they are headed down the path that leads to marital destruction. If you find yourself on that path, I beseech you with all of my heart to abandon that path by no longer doing the things that a husband should never do.

2. Never slap, hit, abuse, or do anything to your wife that brings pain and hurt

It has been said by many ignorant people that, "you must slap a woman to keep her in her place." That is wrong advice, that is sinful advice, and that is advice that may cause your wife to stop loving you. It is also advice that may cause your marriage to end. To slap, hit, abuse, or do anything to cause physical and/or mental hurt to your wife is against the laws of God and men. Doing those things may cause you to be put in jail, it may cause you to have a restraining order levied against you, and it may cause you to be put out of the home. To slap, hit, abuse, or do anything to your wife that causes pain and hurt does more harm to a marriage than any good that you think it may accomplish.

There are many things that can happen in a marriage that is hard for a woman to forget, forgive, and overcome. The pain of abuse is something a wife never forgets; she finds it hard (and almost impossible) to forgive, and she never really gets over it. It stays within her heart for a long time; and in the fullness of time, it shows up by her losing her love for you, her losing her respect for you, and her wishing she were no longer your wife. Abuse also causes your wife to lose her trust in you because, it is hard to trust someone who you know may hurt you.

How can a woman receive pleasure from the intimate part of a marriage when she knows the pain that happens during the times of abuse? How can she make love to a man with her whole heart while thinking, "How can this man lay with me after what he has done to me?"

The pains of abuse not only affect her love for you; it also affects her ability to make love to you. One slap, one hit, or one incident of abuse that brings pain to your wife, will destroy what years of showing her love and doing good things for her have tried to build. Abuse is a powerful tool of destruction.

When you abuse your wife, she thinks that you never really loved her, and that all the so-called good things you did were only lies. She will think, "If he really loved me and if those good things really meant anything, he would never hit me. He can't love me and hit me at the same time."

The true test of what is in a man's heart, most wives think, is what he does when he is angry. If you love your wife, regardless of how angry you get, you will never strike or abuse her. You are to love a wife; and strike an enemy to destroy him to keep him from trying to destroy you. When you strike your wife, you are saying that she is no longer a wife to love but an enemy you must destroy.

God gives you a command to love your wife; He never gives you a command to hit and abuse your wife. God knows what causes a marriage to last and what destroys a marriage. God tells us to do things that will make a marriage last, and He never commands us to do things to destroy our marriage. In the Word of God, you will find many instructions God gives to a husband, but you will never find Him instructing you to strike or abuse your wife.

Your wife is God's daughter (if she is a Christian), and to abuse her will cause God to deal with you in an unpleasant way. Many of the problems you encounter in life may be the result of God dealing with you because of the way you have treated your wife. To mistreat her in any way will evoke the anger of God toward you. To strike or abuse her may cause God to chasten you if you are His child, or bring judgment upon you if you are not His child. The abuse you may inflict upon your wife is not worth the things God may do to you for doing such. God does punish sin, and abuse is sin.

3. Never cheat on your wife

Unfaithfulness is one of the devil's greatest tools to bring havoc and destruction in a marriage. Unfaithfulness causes you to violate your vows to God, to others, to yourself, and to your wife. Unfaithfulness in marriage is something you should never do. Unfaithfulness brings great pain to your wife, and causes her to distrust you in such a way that she may never overcome. The pain of unfaithfulness is hard for a wife to bear. It makes her feel as though she is less than a woman, and as if she is not enough woman for you. It makes her feel that the most sacred thing she has (you) has been defiled. It also makes her feel betrayed. Women feels things much deeper than men, and a husband will never know the depths of the hurt he brings upon his wife when he is unfaithful to her.

No man wants to deal with the hurt and pain of knowing his wife has been unfaithful to him. Because he does not want that pain on himself, he should never put that kind of pain on her. One of the worst things that can happen to a man is to discover his wife has been sleeping with another man. It hurts him so badly that he wants to kill her and the man she has been with. He wants to kick her out of the house and get a divorce. The pain is hard and most unbearable for him. Knowing that is how you would feel about your wife committing adultery against you, should cause you never to commit adultery against her.

Nothing will cause a wife to lose trust in her husband faster than him committing adultery. Once trust is gone, it is hard to rebuild. Every time you are away from her, she will wonder if you are with another woman. When you say you are in one place and for some legitimate reason, you are not there; she will think you lied to her so you could be with another woman. It will take years before she regains her trust in you. You will have to work very hard and give her much time to heal of the hurts and pains. You will have to live your life in such ways that she will know you have totally repented and will never be unfaithful again.

Committing adultery will also cause your wife's love for you to diminish, and it may keep her from ever loving you as a wife should love her husband. Before the adultery, she loved you with all of her heart; but after the adultery, her heart was hurt more than she ever could have imagined. To keep from being hurt like that again, she just refuses to love you with all of her heart. If you value the total love of your wife for you, never be unfaithful to her. <u>Any man can please many women for a short time, but it takes a special man to please one woman (and her only) for a lifetime</u>. Show to yourself, show to your God, and show to your wife that you are a special kind of man. Get so busy loving her that you don't have time to love anyone else. Value her, treasure her, and love her only.

4. Never lie to your wife

The best way never to lie to your wife is to live in such ways that you will do nothing you will have to lie about. Living this kind of life is not always easy, but it is a kind of life that can be lived. If you place your wife above everything and everyone but God, you will live in such ways that you will not do anything to hurt her or betray her. Because you always have her best interest at heart, it will be possible and a little easier to live in such ways that you will not have to lie to her.

Husbands, you should let your speech be seasoned with grace and with truth. Learn to be honest with your wife in everything. If she cooks something you do not like, find a loving way to be honest and tell her you did not like it. She will come to respect your honesty more so than you lying to her to keep from hurting her feelings. When she realizes you are honest in small things, she will realize that you will be honest in all things. Honesty is a virtue you always want in your marriage.

Build your marriage on truth, and your marriage will be a marriage that can last. Build it on lies, and your marriage will not stand. Deception in marriage is a shaky foundation to build upon. My mother always said that I could be sure my lies will find me out. Lies and deceptions in marriage will soon be found out, and will cause problems for your marriage. It will bring distrust and hardships that will have the potential to destroy the marriage. Many problems in marriage can be avoided if the spouses do nothing they will have to lie about, and always be honest with each other.

God tells us not to lie to one another; He tells us to speak the truth in love (Ephesians.4:15). To lie to your wife about anything is to violate the Word of God. It is a sin that not only hurts your wife but angers God. There are six things God hates, and seven are abominations to him. The first is a proud look, and the second is a lying tongue (Proverbs.6:16-17). Never be a part of what God hates. You do not want God's anger in your marriage; you want His grace and blessings in it. In the eyes of God, there is no legitimate reason for you to lie to your wife. Whatever reason you give for lying to her will never stand up before God. Your wife is to be the closest one to you. She is to be the one in whom you confide, and the one who will always be with you to support you. Because of the closeness between you and her, you cannot afford to lie to her, and God will not tolerate you lying to her for any reason.

5. Never embarrass your wife in public or before others

The two ways in which a husband embarrasses his wife in public or before others are; (1) to do something to disgrace her or to make her look bad, and (2) to do something to disgrace himself or to make himself look bad. A wife is very concerned about how she looks in the eyes of others. She will spend hours in the mirror, she will spend large amounts of money at the beauty shop, and she buys the best-looking dresses she can afford because she wants to look her best. When her husband does something to disgrace her in public, it is usually a traumatic experience that brings her great shame and hurt. It also undoes all she has tried to do to make herself look good in the eyes of others.

Not only is a wife concerned about the way she looks, she is also concerned about the way her house looks. She does not want people to come over to her house when it is not clean. She hates it when you bring people over without informing her first. It is not the people she dislikes; it is them coming when her house is not clean. Husbands, always try to let your wife know when you will be bringing company home because, to bring people to her unclean house is an embarrassing experience that brings her shame.

Your wife also hates it when you lay your clothes around everywhere. She hates it when after she has cleaned up, you and the kids come and mess things up. Husbands, help your wife keep the house clean and neat. Make sure the yard is well kept, and if she wants flowers, get them and help her plant them. When you keep the house and yard clean and as beautiful as possible, you are helping to spare her embarrassment.

What you, as her husband, do in public reflects on her as your wife. When you do foolish things in the eyes of others, it makes her feel embarrassed. If you dress in a messy and unattractive way, it embarrasses her. If you live your life in such ways that people speak bad things about you, it brings embarrassment to her. Men are less concerned about what others think or say about them. It does not hurt their feelings, and they are not easily embarrassed about it. Although it does not hurt nor embarrass a man, it does embarrass his wife; therefore, he should watch what he does for his wife's sake.

Husbands, never embarrass your wife before the children. Always treat your wife with love and respect before them. Always say good things about her to them, and do not allow them to say anything bad about her. Demand that they give her the greatest amount of respect possible. She is their mother; and mothers should always receive love, honor, and respect from their children and from their husbands.

Embarrassment is something your wife should never have to deal with. You cannot protect her from all embarrassments, but you can protect her from being embarrassed because of what you do, and because of how you treat her. If you want a good marriage with a wife who loves and respects you, seek never to embarrass her.

Father; thank You for covering me during the times when I fail short. When I did what I was not supposed to do; and I didn't do what I was supposed to do; Your grace covered me. You also worked in my heart giving me wisdom to do the good, while avoiding the bad. I increased in doing good, and totally abandoned doing bad. Now I strive to only do what is right in Your sight. Father; I never would have made it without you.

Jesus my LORD; I have found that Your ways are always the best ways. Thank You for working in the lives of husbands and men in such ways that we avoid doing things which can hurt and destroy our marriages. You are truly the wisdom of our marriages, and You are truly the saving grace of our marriages.

Jesus is LORD

CHAPTER 16

Things That a Husband Should Never Do (Part 2)

6. Never say bad things about your wife.

7. Never discuss with others the things that happen in your bedroom.

8. Never put anyone or anything before your wife but God.

9. Never stop dating your wife.

10. Never stop loving your wife.

6. Never say bad things about your wife.

In the Song of Solomon, wonderful examples are given on the way a husband should talk to and talk about his wife. Although no one is perfect and no one is without some kind of fault, when Solomon saw his wife, she was perfect to him. When he talks about his wife, he has nothing bad to say; in fact, all that he says is good. When he talks to his wife, he only says good things to her. Husbands, be like Solomon in the Song of Solomon, and say only good things to and about your wife.

God says that when a man finds a wife, he finds a good thing. Even with her faults, she is a good thing. Spend your time focusing on her good qualities, and talk only about them. You are not denying the bad; you are just refusing to talk about them. A good rule to follow is talk about her good qualities and pray about her bad qualities. You and she are to notice the bad qualities and work together to overcome them. You can mention the things you think she should change, but never dwell on them, and never make them the major topic of constant discussion.

When talking to your friends and to other people, never say anything bad or demeaning about your wife. They do not need to know any of her negative qualities. Many of the people who ask things about your wife are not out to help you and your marriage; they just want something to talk about to others. Oftentimes, the bad things you say about your wife will eventually get back to her. If you never say anything bad about her, you will never have to regret the things you say about her.

Also, remember that when you say negative things about your wife, you are also saying negative things about yourself. You and your wife are one. To talk about her is to talk about you. Also, to say bad things about her is to say that you don't know how to choose a good wife. It also says you don't know how to take her as she is, and how to work together with her to make a better person out of her. If you really love your wife, refuse to say bad and negative things about her.

7. Never discuss with others the things that happen in your bedroom.

If you are not talking to your doctor or to a professional marriage counselor, do not discuss with others the intimate side of your marriage. The things you and your wife do in private are to remain between you and her. No one, not even your best friend, need to know the details of the intimate affairs that go on between you and your wife. If someone asks you about it, do not be afraid to say to him or her, "This is a personal matter that I refuse to discuss." If your wife finds out you have been telling others about what you and she do in private, she will be embarrassed, she will feel ashamed, and she will be upset with you. It will also affect her performance in the bedroom because she will be reluctant to do anything with you knowing you might tell others. She will also wonder what else you are telling your friends about her and the marriage.

Never tell another woman about the sexual performance of your wife. You should never be so close and friendly with another woman that you feel free to tell her about you and your wife's intimate moments. To talk about sex with another woman is something you should never do because the other woman may be drawn to you sexually as a result of such conversations. If she is not drawn to you sexually, she may spread negative rumors about your wife. There is no legitimate reason for you to talk to another woman about sex, especially the sex that goes on between you and your wife.

When you talk to other men about the sexual activities of you and your wife, it causes their curiosity to be aroused; and they may, as a result, start desiring your wife sexually. If you say she is very good at making love, they may want to find out how good. If you say she is not very good at making love, they may want to teach her how to become good at it. If you say she is not satisfied with you, they may want to see if she will be satisfied with them. They will reason that if she is not satisfied with you, she may be open to getting satisfaction elsewhere. They may then seek to be the person she can come to. Telling others about the sexual affairs of you and your wife does more harm than good, and has the tendency to lead to destructive and sinful behavior. It brings shame on the wife and temptations on the ones you are talking to. Let sex in marriage stay in the bedroom, and never let it be the topic of conversation with others.

8. Never put anyone or anything before your wife but God.

Other than God Himself, your wife is to be the number one person in your life, and nothing and no one is to ever come before her. Many men make the mistake of putting things before their wives. They put before their wives such things as their jobs, their possessions, their friends, their hobbies, their parents, and even other women. To put other people and other things before your wife will cause great problems in your marriage, and will make your wife feel as if she is unimportant to you.

In everything you do, remember your wife comes first. While your wife comes first, there will be times that you will have to say no to her in order to get certain things done. These times should be few, and your wife should understand when this happens. You should live your life in such ways that she knows she is always first. When something comes up that you must do, she should understand because she knows you have a habit of always trying to put her first.

One of the best ways to determine if you are putting your wife first is to ask her if she feels she is first in your life. We as men often think we are putting our wives first when in reality we are not. We say that we work hard, and put in long hours because we want to get nice things for our families. The truth of the matter is that we enjoy being busy and accomplishing things. A sense of accomplishment brings us much satisfaction. Our hard work and long hours are more for our egos than they are for our families.

Another way to put your wife first is to always do things with her and for her that makes her happy and content. Develop hobbies that the family, she, and you can do together. Plan for those hobbies, and push other things aside in order to accomplish doing things with her and the family. These things must be done constantly and consistently, but they are not to be the same things every time. When your wife sees that you are dedicating special times for her and the family, she may not mind the hard work and the long hours.

Another way to make your wife feel she is first is to discuss things with her that is happening in your life. Tell her about things on the job as well as the things you and your friends do. Invite her into your world at times so she will know she is a part of it. Take her on the job if you can. Take her on fishing trips, hunting trips, basketball games, golf games, etc., with you and your friends.

Also, come and share in her world with her by doing things she likes to do. It is usually not the work you do nor the friends you spend time with that makes her feel as if she is second in your life. What makes her feel as if she is second is that you do not give her enough of your personal time; and you do not tell her what is happening in your world. A wise man is one who has learned to spend quality time with his wife and family, even if he must spend quantities of time with career. He has even learned how to make his family feel they are a part of his career and are more important than his career.

The special quality times you spend with your wife and family are great, but the special moments you dedicate to your wife are treasures of lasting value that shall never be taken away. Special moments are when you call her during the day just to say hello. It is the time when you call to say, "I was thinking about you, so I decided to call to tell you I love you." Special moments are the cards, candies, and flowers sent for no special reason. Special moments are the notes of love left for her. Special moments are the special little things you do to show you love her. Never neglect spending special quality time with your wife, and always take time out to perform the special moments of love that will let your wife know she is first in your life.

Your wife will also feel she is first when you put the children before your career, hobbies, and friends. Remember there should also be special times for them and special moments for them. Call and talk to the kids when you know you will be late coming home. Go and buy your children toys, CDs, and other gifts to let them know you think about them during the day. Bring pizza and soda home every now and then. Plan special outings for them and be involved in their school activities and in other activities they may be involved in. Putting your wife and family first is really a matter of what you do to show them you love them and are thinking about them constantly.

9. Never stop dating your wife.

Someone once said, "What it took to get your wife, it will take the same thing to keep her." The truth of the matter is, what it took to get your wife, it will take the same things *and much more* to keep her (i.e., to keep her happy and content). Never allow dating and romance to leave your marriage. Those things convinced her to marry you, and those are the things that will convince her to stay married to you. Never decrease romance after marriage; increase it. Romance in marriage is not something that happens automatically. It must be planned and then worked at. It will take imagination, time, and energy. If you as a husband want your marriage to be the best it can be, you must do your best at romancing your wife, and dating your wife.

When romance and dating leave, routine and boredom set in. Oftentimes, after a man gets married, he becomes so caught up in providing for the family, raising children, repairing the home, yard work, cleaning the garage, and other things, that he forgets and neglects the romantic and feminine side of his wife. After a while, his wife becomes frustrated with home, family, and responsibilities. We need to always do things that will let our wives know that although they are mothers and wives, they are still beautiful women worthy of being romanced and dated by us.

10. Never stop loving your wife.

Love is something that must be maintained. You as a husband must do things that will cause you to always love your wife, and to always let it show. Don't depend on her doing things to keep you interested in her and loving her. There will be times when she will do nothing to help you to love her. She may even do things that will try to cause you to stop loving her. You loving your wife is something you have to continually work at if your love for her is going to remain.

The major reason to never stop loving your wife is because God commanded you to love her. If you cannot love her for her, you should be able to love her for Jesus. If you love God enough to obey Him in everything, you will always love your wife because loving your wife is part of obeying the commands of God. <u>To never stop loving your wife, you must focus on her good qualities, give her grace for her bad qualities, and always work to help her improve and get better.</u>

To stop loving your wife is a sin against God, a wrong done to her, and a devastating hurt that you place on your children. It costs you more not to love your wife than it does for you to love her. Not loving your wife hurts the kingdom of Christ because it is Christ who wants our marriages to be a reflection of the relationship of Him and the church. Also, it is a great injustice to a woman to live with a man who she knows does not love her. It brings her heartaches and tears, and it makes her feel less than a woman.

Not loving your wife also inflicts great suffering on your children. They live with the fear of thinking their mother and father may end their marriage. They fear that if you no longer love their mother, you may eventually stop loving them. If the marriage ends, it brings greater hurt and agony on them than it does on you or your wife. The children may feel it is their fault that the marriage came to an end, and they will blame themselves.

To stop loving your wife is a sin that brings great pain and suffering to God, your wife, your children, and yourself. There is no pain like the pain of losing a good wife and then, years later, realizing it was your own fault. If she remarries and finds a new husband that treats her with love and respect, you will be hurt and will always regret it. As a husband, you must realize it is better to continue loving your wife than it is to stop loving her and thus sin against God. It hurts you more than it does anyone else when you stop loving your wife. So, husband, continue loving your wife and continue showing love to her.

God's Divine Instructions To Husbands and Men

Father; eternal love. Thank You. In Jesus' name I pray; amen.

Jesus my LORD; Thank You for Your never ending love.

Jesus is LORD

CHAPTER 17

A Word to Those Who Have Been Divorced and Remarried

1. A Word to Those Who Have Been Divorced and Remarried

2. Biblical Reasons for Divorce
   A. A person can divorce their spouse if their spouse commits adultery.
   B. A person can divorce their spouse if their spouse leaves them or forces them to leave.
   C. If there is physical and mental abuse, you may leave your wife and divorce her.
   D. If your wife is involved in continuous abominable (sinful) living and refuse to repent, you can divorce her.

3. Biblical Consequences of Divorce

4. What a Divorced and Remarried Person Should Do
   A. When you have been divorced for a reason given in the Bible and you are not the one at fault, you can remarry in the Lord with God's blessings
   B. If you have experienced a divorce for a none biblical reason (and you and your wife have not been remarried), you need to confess your sins to God, begin living your life totally for Jesus, and then seek to be reconciled to your spouse.
   C. If you have been divorced and remarried for none biblical reasons but it happened before you came into the knowledge of what God

says about marriage, divorce, and remarriage, you and your new spouse can receive forgiveness because of your not knowing

D. If you knew what God said about marriage, divorce, and remarriage but you divorce for a none biblical reason and remarried, you and your spouse are living in adultery.
E. If you are married and are contemplating a divorce for a none biblical reason, don't tempt God by getting a divorce.
F. If you are in a troubled marriage and it seems to be no one's fault and things are just not working out right, you still are not entitled to get a divorce.

5. Overcoming the Pains of Divorce

Aelton Simmons

1. A word to those who have been divorced and remarried

Our society is filled with men who have been married, divorced, and remarried. Many of them have become Christians after their divorce and remarriage occurred, while many were Christians already. Because they are Christians, they want to know what God says about divorce and remarriage. While there are many things the Bible says about divorce and remarriage, we will deal with three major aspects of it. We will deal with:

1. Biblical reasons for divorce,
2. The biblical consequence that happens to a divorced person and others.
3. What a divorced and remarried person should do.

In the course of this chapter, we will also be touching on many other subjects that will be of vital importance to all men. Our aim is not to condemn but to educate, encourage, and inspire those who have gone through such unpleasant experiences, or may be going through such unpleasant experiences now.

2. Biblical Reasons for Divorce

It is God's desire for marriages to last a lifetime; however, God does allow for divorce but only under certain conditions and circumstances. Biblical reasons for divorce are (1) adultery, (2) abandonment, (3) abuse, and (4) abominable (sinful) living. While God does allow divorce because of these reasons, He would prefer couples to repent of their sins, forgive each other, and work on making the marriage continue and improve. Reconciliation is His major desire for a troubled marriage, but if reconciliation is deemed impossible and/or undesirable by the couple, divorce is permitted but only for reasons given in the Holy Bible.

God's Divine Instructions To Husbands and Men

A. A person can divorce their spouse if their spouse commits adultery.

⁹· *And I say unto you, Whosoever shall put away his wife, except it be for fornication, and shall marry another, committeth adultery: and whoso marrieth her which is put away doth commit adultery. (Matthew.19:9)*

If a spouse commits adultery, God would prefer for the other spouse to forgive their spouse and work on causing the marriage to continue. If your wife is committing adultery and refuses to repent of her adultery, then you are free to divorce her, and you will be held guiltless before God. You are then free to marry someone else in the Lord. (You may need to review the section of this book entitled "Bitterness Because of Adultery.")

B. A person can divorce their spouse if their spouse leaves them or forces them to leave.

¹⁰*And unto the married I command, yet not I, but the Lord, Let not the wife depart from her husband:* ¹¹*But and if she depart, let her remain unmarried, or be reconciled to her husband: and let not the husband put away his wife.* ¹²*But to the rest speak I, not the Lord: If any brother hath a wife that believeth not, and she be pleased to dwell with him, let him not put her away.* ¹³*And the woman which hath an husband that believeth not, and if he be pleased to dwell with her, let her not leave him.* ¹⁴*For the unbelieving husband is sanctified by the wife, and the unbelieving wife is sanctified by the husband: else were your children unclean; but now are they holy.* ¹⁵ **But if the unbelieving depart, let him depart. A brother or a sister is not under bondage in such cases: but God hath called us to peace.** *(1ˢᵗ Corinthians.7:10-15)*

If your wife walks out and leaves you (and it is no fault of your own) and she refuses to return, you can divorce her and be held guiltless before God. If she forces you to leave (by a court order or by some other means) and you are not at fault, you can leave and divorce her and be held guiltless in the eyes of God. You can go and marry someone else in the Lord.

C. If there is physical and mental abuse, you may leave your wife and divorce her.

Oftentimes, in the scriptures, when the life and health of Jesus was threatened, He had to withdraw Himself (Matthew. 12:14-15; Luke 4:28-30; John 8:59).

And all they in the synagogue, when they heard these things, were filled with wrath, And rose up, and thrust him out of the city, and led him unto the brow of the hill whereon their city was built, that they might cast him down headlong. **But he passing through the midst of them went his way.** *(Luke 4:28-30)*

When you and the children are in physical or mental danger because of your wife, you may leave her. If she maintains an abusive attitude toward you and toward the children, and she refuses to get professional help for her problem, you may seek a divorce.

D. If your wife is involved in continuous abominable (sinful) living and refuse to repent, you can divorce her.

If your spouse is living in the kinds of wickedness described in 1st Corinthians.5:11-13, and she refuses to repent, you may put her away from you.

[11] But now I have written unto you not to keep company, if any man that is called a brother be a fornicator, or covetous, or an idolater, or a railer, or a drunkard, or an extortioner; with such an one no not to eat. [12] For what have I to do to judge them also that are without? do not ye judge them that are within? [13] But them that are without God judgeth. **Therefore put away from among yourselves that wicked person.** *(1st Corinthians.5:11-13)*

These kinds of wickedness not only hurt the spouse who is doing these things; they also have the potential of destroying the other spouse and the children. There are some alcoholics who beat and abuse their spouses and children, drug addicts can be dangerous, and extortion is illegal. If your spouse is involved in these things (or other things of this nature) and refuses to repent, she is dangerous to herself and to her family, thus you may need to separate yourself from her.

3. Biblical consequences of divorce

If a person gets a divorce for a none biblical reason, the consequences they must face are as follows: (1) they commit adultery, (2) the person they marry next is committing adultery, (3) they have broken the covenant God established for a husband and wife in marriage, and (4) it causes them to forfeit many of the blessings God had for them.

When a person divorces his or her spouse for a none biblical reason and marry someone else, they, in the eyes of God, are living in adultery (Matthew.19:9). When a man and woman unites in marriage, God unites them as one. Only God can separate a married couple; however, He only separates them for reasons given in the Holy Bible. When they go before a judge and gets a divorce (and it is for none biblical reasons), God does not accept the divorce; and in His eyes, if they remarry, they are committing adultery because God sees them as still married to the first spouse. Men may have separated them, but God did not separate them.

When a person marries someone who has been divorced for none biblical reasons, they are marrying someone whom God sees as another person's spouse. They take another person's spouse and call them their own, but in God's eyes, that spouse is not theirs; he or she is someone else's. Many men are living with another man's wife and are calling her his own. Many wives are living with another woman's husband and are calling him her own. When you marry a person who has been divorced for none biblical reasons, you can call him or her what you may, but God calls him or her and you adulterers. (However, God calling you and her an adulterer can be changed. Read the section called "What a Divorced and Remarried Person Should Do.")

God holds covenant agreements as sacred, and the most sacred covenant of all is the covenant that occurs when a man and a woman enters into marriage. It is a covenant they make with each other as well as with God. They make promises to each other as well as to God. To break that covenant with each other is to break it with God.

¹⁴ Yet ye say, Wherefore? Because the LORD hath been witness between thee and the wife of thy youth, against whom thou hast dealt treacherously: yet is she thy companion, and the wife of thy covenant. ¹⁵ And did not he make one? Yet had he the residue of the spirit. And wherefore one? That he might seek a godly seed. Therefore take heed to your spirit, and let none deal treacherously against the wife of his youth. ¹⁶ **For the LORD, the God of Israel, saith that he hateth putting away:** *for one covereth violence with his garment, saith the LORD of hosts: therefore take heed to your spirit, that ye deal not treacherously.* (Malachi.2:14-16)

God sees the marriage covenant as a spiritual thing being violated when a divorce happens, and He may deal harshly with the one at fault. You can't break the covenant of God without God dealing with you about it. Always remember that when a person considers getting a divorce, they need to first consider what God says about it.

When a man and a woman unites in marriage, they become joint heirs of the grace of life. There are certain great and wonderful blessings they can only receive when they are married to each other. When they divorce from each other, they forfeit those blessings and thus fall short of the best God has for them. The spouse that is at fault will never be as blessed as they could have been if they would have remained married. The one who is not at fault may receive greater blessings, but the one at fault may have lost some of the best blessings God had in store for him/her in this life.

4. What a divorced and remarried person should do

A. *When you have been divorced for a reason given in the Bible and you are not the one at fault, you can remarry in the Lord with God's blessings.*

When you as a spouse have done your best in the marriage and the marriage still does not work, do not be laden with guilt and shame. You can take comfort in knowing you have done your best, and then realize God is well pleased with you for trying your best. Then go forward in life, knowing God still has greater blessings in store for you. You may be experiencing hurt and heartache now, but in the fullness of time, God will replace them with joy and love. *God has better days ahead for you.*

B. *If you have experienced a divorce for a none biblical reason (and you and your wife have not been remarried), you need to confess your sins to God, begin living your life totally for Jesus, and then seek to be reconciled to your spouse.*

The first thing a person should do when they realize they have sinned is to confess the sin to God and then repent of the sin. Tell God in prayer of the sins you have committed in your marriage, and then ask for His forgiveness. If at all possible, seek to be reconciled to your spouse. Reconciliation will take time and much work, but if you and your spouse can reconcile, it will be well worth it.

If reconciliation is deemed impossible and your spouse refuses to take you back, you can go and be remarried, but you are to only marry a Christian woman. Once your spouse refuses to take you back, you are then free of the old marriage and can now remarry. If your spouse is willing to take you back but you refuse to go back, you must remain unmarried (1st Corinthians.7:10-11). To marry someone else when your spouse would have taken you back will cause you and the person you are marrying to live in adultery.

C. *If you have been divorced and remarried for none biblical reasons but it happened before you came into the knowledge of what God says about marriage, divorce, and remarriage; you and your new spouse can receive forgiveness because of your not knowing.*

[13] *Who was before a blasphemer, and a persecutor, and injurious: but I obtained mercy, because I did it ignorantly in unbelief. (1st Timothy.1:13.)*

Confess the sin to God; ask for His forgiveness, and He will grant it. He will also begin blessing you and your new marriage. Live in that new marriage according to the Word and will of God from this day forward. God is a God of great mercy, grace, and forgiveness. God is a God who specializes in giving people another chance.

D. *If you knew what God said about marriage, divorce, and remarriage; but you divorce for a none biblical reason and remarried, you and your spouse are living in adultery.*

Also, you have tempted God because you, knowing what He said about divorce and remarriage, committed the sin anyway. However, you are not to divorce your new spouse and try to return to your first. That would be a greater sin than the first. The best you can do is to cry out to God asking for His forgiveness and grace (He is a merciful God). Ask Him to wipe away your reproach and to cleanse you in the blood of Jesus Christ His son. After confessing your sins to God, begin living your life totally for Jesus Christ. Treat your new spouse as the Holy Bible says to treat her, and God may cause the marriage to be its best.

E. *If you are married and are contemplating a divorce for a none biblical reason, don't tempt God by getting a divorce.*

You know what God says about the matter, and you have full understanding on the subject of divorce and remarriage. It is not time to tempt God; it is time to trust God and to obey what He says about marriage. Make sure you are doing what you are supposed to do in the marriage. Seek God in prayer, and then work to overcome any and all problems. It is worse to tempt God by getting a divorce for a non-biblical reason than it is to believe God and stay in the marriage, even if things are hard for you and her. The results of tempting God are far worse than living in a troubled marriage while trusting God for victory. We must believe and remember God can straighten out a troubled marriage and bless it.

F. *If you are in a troubled marriage and it seems to be no one's fault and things are just not working out right, you still are not entitled to get a divorce.*

When things are not working well in a marriage, someone is always at fault. Someone (if not both spouses) is not doing what God instructed him or her to do. If things are not working out very well in your marriage right now, it is time for you to start obeying what God instructs a husband to do so that things can start getting better in your marriage. Develop the mental attitude that when things are not right in your marriage, you will not seek a divorce, but you will seek God for solutions and victories.

If you are fulfilling your God-given responsibilities in the marriage but your wife is not fulfilling her God-given responsibilities, you still do not have a right to get a divorce. If she is pleased to stay married to you and she is not doing any of the things the Holy Bible says you can get a divorce for, you are to remain married to her. You are not to stop fulfilling your duties, but you are to do as much for her as God says and as much as she will allow you. Constantly pray and believe God for the marriage to improve and for your wife to start fulfilling her God-given duties as a wife. Do not enter into sin, and stay away from committing adultery and/or engaging in illicit affairs. Do not allow a root of bitterness to spring up within you, and remember to overcome any bad situation by doing good things. Always remember that love covers a multitude of faults, even the faults of your spouse.

5. Overcoming the pains of divorce

Two of the greatest pains that a man can experience in this life are (1) the pains of losing a very close loved one (parents, spouse, children, etc.) through death and (2) the pains that accompany a divorce. Divorce is a painful experience that has the potential of leaving emotional scars that can last a lifetime. Divorce brings hurts, wounds, regrets, sorrows, and sadness. It also brings deep feelings of betrayal and abandonment. Divorce is a horrible thing that many men are trying to cope with. They have lost their wives, they have been separated from their children, and they now must go through the hassle of starting over again.

While many women think men are hard-hearted creatures devoid of feelings and emotions, many divorced men are crying out, asking for help in dealing with their gut-wrenching pain. These men feel lost and confused. They really do not know what to do; nor do they know how to cope with the overwhelming devastating emotions of hurt, sadness, and loneliness that floods their souls. They are lost in a world that appears out of their control; and they are helpless to change times, circumstances, and events. In their darkened world of despair, they desperately cry out asking, "Is there any help and comfort for me from the pains of divorce?"

How does one overcome the pains of divorce? How does one deal with the reality of being a victim of divorce? How does one bounce back stronger, wiser, and better? How does one go forward in life when he feels he has failed so miserably? **To overcome the pains of divorce, you must first come to the realization that although your marriage may be over, your life does not have to be.** Instead of seeing divorce as a tragic end, see it as a bad experience you encountered on the road of your life as you journey from its beginning to its physical end. The experience may have come because of faults on your part or because of a combination of adverse situations and circumstances that may have been out of your control. Regardless of the cause, you experienced it, and it is now time to go forward on the road of the rest of your life.

As you go forward on the road of life after a divorce, there will be many hurdles and obstacles to overcome. **The greatest of these obstacles are the mental and emotional battles you must fight within yourself.** The mental battles of thinking and feeling that you are a failure and that you (in the eyes of a woman) are not worth living with, are mental battles you must fight. The emotional battles of trying to rise above your feelings of being hurt, abandoned, and forsaken, will come often. Although these battles will come, you will (if you trust in God) rise above them and come out victoriously with joy and peace in your heart.

However, when these battles come, you must believe that while you are fighting many battles (and you may even lose a few), you will eventually win the war. You must hold on to the hopes of believing God will see you through and that He will comfort and strengthen you. Realize also that during your times of battle you will experience hurt and pain. You will experience these feelings because it is impossible not to have such feelings after a divorce.

Along with the feelings of hurt and pain, **you will spend many hours regretting many of the things that happened, and you will spend many**

sleepless nights wishing you had not done some of the things you did. Learn to properly deal with those feelings and thoughts, and do not let them destroy you. Use those feelings as instruments of learning that eventually make a better person out of you. While you cannot change the past and while you may not be able to correct the mistakes of the past, refuse to allow the past to destroy you, to destroy your present, and to destroy your future.

If you tried to walk forward while looking backward, you may end up in a ditch (or someplace worse). **To overcome the pains of divorce, begin to look forward in life.** You are looking forward in life when you begin preparing for the future, however, you are looking backward when you are constantly regretting the past. Start concentrating on how to go forward in life. Begin making goals to accomplish and plans to achieve. See your life as a new challenge filled with exciting and wonderful possibilities. Have faith in your heart that, with God's grace and blessings, your today and your tomorrows will be better, and will be more blessed than your yesterdays were. Look forward to the good things God will bring with your tomorrows while seeking to overcome the pains of your yesterdays.

When seeking to go forward after a divorce, remember to include your children as part of your wonderful tomorrows. Plan to spend as much time with them as possible. Do not make plans for your life and then include your children; make plans for your children first, and then plan your life around the plans you have for your children. A few months after a divorce, many men exit the lives of their children, never to return. They spend little time with them and even less money on them. These men are so busy trying to rebuild their lives, they usually do not take time out to build their children.

Fathers, even though you may no longer be in the house with your children, you still have a responsibility to try to develop your children into the best people they can be. You may not be able to spend large quantities of time with them, but make the times you do spend with them maximum quality time. When making your plans and schedules, you should begin by first making plans that include being with your children and doing fun things with and for them. After those plans are set, all other plans are to be scheduled around those times. Always make your children your greatest priority. Cancel other things so you can be with your children, and make it a habit not to cancel being with your children so you can do other things.

As a divorced husband, not only will you feel the pains of divorce, your children will feel them as well. <u>Instead of seeking someone to comfort you, spend much time comforting your children.</u> Reassure them that the divorce was not their fault, and they are never to feel guilty about it. Let them know that although the marriage ended, your love and devotion to them will never end. Tell them that they are still a part of your heart and life and that you will always be available for them. <u>The divorced spouses often talk about the pains they feel, but they fail to realize their children will be the ones to feel the greatest pain as a result of the divorce.</u>

After a divorce, your children will need more love, affection, time, and attention than they did before the divorce. They will constantly need to be reassured of your love for them, and it must show in the things you say and in the things you do. It must show in the amount of time you spend with them and the number of times you call to check on them. Allow them to go through and express some negative emotions without you showing anger and without you trying to immediately correct them. Let them cry on your shoulder. Let them vent their frustrations and hurts at times. Let them unburden their souls. They are hurting deeply just as you are, and they truly need to express that hurt at times.

<u>When your divorced wife seeks to rebuild her life with another man, you must not interfere with that, and you must guard against being angry and hurt.</u> You must not allow yourself to dwell on the thoughts of "Why is she able to make it with him and not with me?" What has happened, just happened, and what is now happening is outside of your control. As earlier stated, <u>it's now time to take your eyes off of what she is doing and focus on what God will do for you and for your life</u>. Her life is now in the hands of God; therefore, allow Him to do in her life as he wills.

Also, remember that God may, in the fullness of time, bring someone into your life; and you too will begin to build a new life with another. When going through the devastation of divorce, focus on God, focus on your life, and focus on your children. Overcome all negative thinking, put the past behind you, pray for strength and wisdom, and strive to go forward in life with a positive attitude and with great expectations for the future.

Father; the only way to rebound from the negative and devastating affairs of life is to keep our eyes on You. We must trust You, depend on You, and obey You. Prayer must be a constant part of our lives, and we must believe You will work all things together for our good and for Your glory. We must be patient and wait on You. You will renew our strength. In Jesus' name I pray; amen.

[13] I had fainted, unless I had believed to see the goodness of the LORD in the land of the living. [14] Wait on the LORD: be of good courage, and he shall strengthen thine heart: wait, I say, on the LORD. (Psalms.27:13-14).

[28] And we know that all things work together for good to them that love God, to them who are the called according to his purpose. (Romans.8:28)

Jesus my LORD; through Your redemptive work on the Cross, we have victory over everything we encounter in life. Thank you for giving us the Holy Ghost to anoint us, and to empower us to live in victory even during times of divorce.

Jesus is LORD

CHAPTER 18

What Is a Man, and What Is a Man Supposed to Do?

1. Three different views to consider.
   A. The first view a person can use to define what a man is and what a man is supposed to do is what people and society says.
   B. The second view that a person can use to define what a man is and what a man is supposed to do is his personal opinions.
   C. The third view a person can use to define what a man is and what a man is supposed to do is God's view as found in the Holy Bible.

2. A man is to be a reflection (image) of God (Genesis.1:27, 5:1-2, Romans.8:29).
   A. In order to become the reflection of God, a person must first become a Christian.
   B. After becoming a Christian, in order for a man to become a reflection of God, he must grow in his knowledge of God and in his obedience to Christ.
   C. In order to become a reflection of God, a man must also be living a lifestyle of doing good works.
   D. In order to become the image and reflection of God, a man must allow the fruit of the Spirit to constantly grow in him.

3. A man is to be a person of dominion and authority (Genesis.1:26-28, 1st Corinthians. 11:3, Hebrews.2:6-8).
   A. A man is to have dominion and authority over himself.

B. A man is to have dominion and authority over his own home.
   C. A man, if he is married with children, is to have dominion and authority over his wife and family.

4. A man is to be a person that works (Genesis.3:19, 2nd Thessalonians.3:10, Ephesians.4:28).
   A. A man is to work for money so he can provide for his own.
   B. A man is to always do good works that show he is a child of God.
   C. A man is to work at home.
   D. A man is to also work on raising his children in the nurture and admonition of the Lord.
   E. A man is to work on himself.

Aelton Simmons

1. Three different views to consider

Life is filled with a multitude of questions that people need to ponder and ask themselves. There are questions about salvation, questions of whether to marry or not to marry, and questions on the meaning of life. There are questions about careers to pursue, life goals to accomplish, and family values to achieve. Some questions will be easy to answer, some questions will be hard to answer, and some questions should not be answered at all. With all of the questions to be asked and all of the answers to be given, there are two questions that every man should add to his list of questions that must be answered. These two questions are (1) what is a man? and (2) what is a man supposed to do?

When seeking to define what a man is and what a man is supposed to do, a person can consider three views:

> *A. The first view a person can use to define what a man is, and what a man is supposed to do, is what people and society says.*

The problem with seeking people's and society's view is that people and society have so many different opinions to what a man is and what a man is supposed to do; the person seeking to know will become more confused than anything else. Another problem with people's and society's views is that their views are constantly changing. Their views change so much that when a person becomes what someone says they should be, people's views will change again, and the person will soon find himself outdated and must change. The person will then find himself constantly changing and will never know what his final outcome will be. Thus, using people's and society's view to define what a man is and what a man is supposed to do will leave a person confused and in a state of constant change that leads to uncertainty.

> *B. The second view that a person can use to define what a man is, and what a man is supposed to do, is his personal opinions.*

The problem with using one's personal opinions is that it may lead to many harmful and diverse lusts. These lusts have the potential to destroy him (and others) physically, mentally, and spiritually. One's personal opinions may lead them to homosexuality, which, in my opinion, is a destructive behavior physically, mentally, and spiritually. One's personal opinions may lead them to immorality, which may cause many children to be born out of wedlock, or may be a contributing factor to many abortions. Immorality may lead to sexually transmitted disease, broken homes, and devastated children.

Another problem with using one's personal opinions to define what a man is, and what a man is supposed to do is, that it may infringe on the rights of other people. Rape, crime, violence, child molestation, and other hideous acts are by-products of one's personal opinions. Using one's personal opinions to define what a man is and what a man is supposed to do lead more toward destructive behavior than toward anything else.

> *C. The third view a person can use to define what a man is, and what a man is supposed to do, is God's view as found in the Holy Bible.*

God's view is the same for everyone and does not change with time. God's view does not lead to harmful and diverse lusts that will destroy a person physically, mentally, and spiritually. God's view does not cause one person to infringe on the rights of others in a harmful way. When seeking to define what a man is and what a man is supposed to do, the wisest thing a person can do is to study the Word of God, and use God's views and instructions as their final basis of authority. While there are many different views on what a man is and what a man is supposed to do, God's view is always the best view and is the only right view.

2. A man is to be a reflection (image) of God (Genesis. 1:27, 5:1-2, Romans. 8:29).

God created man to be a reflection of Himself. For a natural-born male to become the type of man God desires, he must seek to be as much a reflection of God as possible. It is to be noted that in order for a person to become a man, he must be born a male. One cannot be born a female and later become a man. The physical surgery a person goes through to become another gender does not alter God's classification of them as being the gender in which they were born. God makes no mistakes. He does not put a female in a male's body so she can later be converted into a man.

Today, one may be able to alter their gender physically, and may go through some personality changes, but it does not cause God to alter his classification of them being the gender in which they were born. Wearing women's clothes, changing the sound of one's voice in an attempt to make it sound like a female, and imitating the actions of a female does not, in God's eyes, make a man a woman, nor does doing the opposite makes a woman a man.

While God does not change His classification of a person's gender, He does not hate those who may be transvestites or homosexuals. God hates the sin, but He does not hate the one committing the sin. God reaches out to them with His love, desiring them to be converted to Christianity. Once converted, God wants them to alter their lifestyle into that which is according to the Holy Bible. One is not condemned to hell because of being a transvestite or homosexual; they are condemned to hell only for rejecting Jesus Christ as the Lord and Savior of their life. However, if a person does accept Jesus Christ as Lord, they should repent of the sinful behavior of being a transvestite or homosexual (or whatever sinful habits they are involved in) and seek to become the reflection of God that the Bible calls them to be.

Know ye not that the unrighteous shall not inherit the kingdom of God? Be not deceived: neither fornicators, nor idolaters, nor adulterers, nor effeminate, nor abusers of themselves with mankind, Nor thieves, nor covetous, nor drunkards, nor revilers, nor extortioners, shall inherit the kingdom of God. **_And such were some of you: but ye are washed, but ye are sanctified, but ye are justified in the name of the Lord Jesus, and by the Spirit of our God._** *(1st Corinthians.6:9-11)*

Man was created in the image of God, but sin came into the world, and men were changed into the image of the devil.

⁴⁴ Ye are of your father the devil, and the lusts of your father ye will do. He was a murderer from the beginning, and abode not in the truth, because there is no truth in him. When he speaketh a lie, he speaketh of his own: for he is a liar, and the father of it. (John 8:44)

If a man desires to be the type of man God wants him to be, he must work to once again become a reflection of God.

> *A. In order to become the reflection of God, a man must first become a Christian (Romams.10:9-10).*

He must believe in his heart that Jesus Christ is the only begotten son of God who died on the Cross for the sins of the world, and that three days later, God raised him from the dead. Then he must confess with his mouth that he wants Jesus to forgive him of his sins, and come into his heart to be his Lord and Savior. Believing and confessing leads to salvation.

> *B. After becoming a Christian, in order for him to become a reflection of God, he must grow in his knowledge of God and in his obedience to Christ.*

It is the desire of God that His children be spiritually mature. If a man is going to become spiritually mature, he must study the Word of God constantly. He needs to attend church, Sunday school, and Bible study. If he hungers and thirsts after righteousness, he shall be filled, and he also will become spiritually mature. As a man begins to grow spiritually and puts into practice the things he has learned, he will begin to act more and more like God. He will begin doing those things that are right and just, he will begin to love everyone, and he will begin to become more compassionate and merciful. He will begin doing these things because these are the things God does. When people see him, they will notice the change within his life and will be able to see God in him. The reason they will be able to see God in him is because he is becoming the image and reflection of God.

> *C. In order to become a reflection of God, he must also be living a lifestyle of doing good works.*

[16] *Let your light so shine before men, that they may see your good works, and glorify your Father which is in heaven. (Matthew.5:16)*

It is through good works that people will see the light of Christ within him and glorify his Father who is in heaven. God is a God who always does good things for people, and if a man is going to be a reflection and image of God, he must be a man who is always doing good works. It is to be noted that he is not doing good works to try to earn salvation; he is doing good works because he is saved and is trying to show it. God is not asking the unsaved to do good works; He is asking them to get saved first (by accepting Jesus Christ as their Lord and Savior) and then begin doing good works that will glorify Him. Good works are not a means to salvation; they show that one is already saved and that God is their Father.

A sinner who does good works (or good things for and to people) is not a reflection of God because to become a reflection of God, one must be in God. Sinners are not in God; thus, they cannot be a reflection of God. Also, the good works that a sinner does glorifies (1) himself, (2) someone else, or (3) a cause; however, the good works they do does not glorify God. The difference between the good works of a sinner and the good works of a saint is that the good works of the sinner does not glorify God, while the good works of a saint is to the glory of God the Father and Jesus Christ his son.

> D. *In order to become the image and reflection of God, a man must allow the fruit of the Spirit to constantly grow in him.*

[22] *But the fruit of the Spirit is love, joy, peace, longsuffering, gentleness, goodness, faith,* [23] *Meekness, temperance: against such there is no law. (Galatians.5:22-23)*

If the Spirit of God is in you, it will show up within your personality and within your life. You will abandon the works of the flesh and constantly seek to walk in the fruit of the Spirit. If you say you are a Christian, you will reflect the things of God. If you reflect the works of the flesh, it is a clear indication that (1) you may not be saved, (2) you are not an image and reflection of God, and (3) you are not the type of man God says a man ought to be. If a man fails in making an attempt of being a reflection of God, he will fail in meeting God's definition of a man. The person may be considered a man by society and by the fact that he is too old to be called a boy; but in the eyes of God, while he is a man to others, he is not the type of man God says a man should be.

3. A man is to be a person of dominion and authority (Genesis. 1:26-28, 1st Corinthians. 11:3, Hebrews. 2:6-8).

God has made the human race to be creatures of dominion and authority. He commanded men to have dominion over His earthly creation and over His earthly creatures. God gave Adam dominion and authority over the Garden of Eden. In Genesis 2:15, Adam was to dress the garden (make it look beautiful), and he was to keep it (take care of it and make sure everything in the garden is as it should be). A man will not be the kind of man God wants him to be until he becomes a man of dominion and authority.

Dominion and authority refers to an area in which a person has rule over. It is an area in which he makes the rules and sets the guidelines for others to follow. It is an area where he has the responsibility of watching over, taking care of, and ensuring the proper operation of. It is an area where he is in control. The rules and guidelines he set can be those that have been established by someone else or by himself. The saved man should never make his own rules to govern the areas in which he has dominion and authority over; he just implements the rules God has already established for him to follow.

While God created men to be creatures of dominion and authority, they must realize that they are also creatures that are to be under dominion and authority. The ultimate authority over every man should be Jesus Christ. No man can properly exercise dominion and authority until he first comes under the dominion and authority of Jesus Christ.

Are you under the dominion and authority of Jesus Christ, or are you under the dominion and authority of the devil? All men are born sinners and, therefore, are subject to the devil's authority. When they accept Jesus Christ as the Lord and Savior of their lives, they come from under the authority of the devil, and comes under the authority of Christ. As long as a man is under the devil's authority, he will never be the type of man God says a man should be. When a person leaves Satan's authority by coming to Christ, they are then free to exercise the proper dominion and authority God has given to every saved man.

A. A man is to have dominion and authority over himself.

He should be able to control (by the power of the Holy Ghost) his own actions.

*¹ I beseech you therefore, brethren, by the mercies of God, that ye present your bodies a living sacrifice, holy, acceptable unto God, **which is your reasonable service.** ². And be not conformed to this world: but be ye transformed by the renewing of your mind, that ye may prove what is that good, and acceptable, and perfect, will of God. (Romans. 12:1-2)*

When confronted with the temptations of this life, he should be able to exercise dominion and authority over himself, and turn down sinful temptations. When he is supposed to do something but does not feel like doing it, he should have enough control over himself to make himself do it anyway. The first area of dominion and authority a man is to have, is authority over himself. If he cannot rule over himself, he will not be able to properly rule over others.

B. A man is to have dominion and authority over his own home.

Every adult man should have his own home or apartment in which he has total dominion and authority over. He is to be able to establish the rules and guidelines that will govern his home. Those rules and guidelines, however, are not to be in violation of the written Word of God. Some men have more than their homes in which they exercise dominion and authority over. They have dominion and authority over their job, community, city, state, nation, and other areas where they have been granted authority to bear rule. When it comes to having dominion and authority, some men have many areas in which they have authority over, while others have only a few areas in which they have authority over; but all men, who are godly men, should at least have two areas; himself and his home.

Every man should at least have a home to rule. He may be a servant on his job and a servant in other organizations, but in his home, he is to be the ruler. His home may not be the best-looking home or the biggest home in town, but it is his home, and he is to be the king there. Because a man's home is his castle, in which he is the king, he should strive to make it the best it can be and the cleanest it can be. He should make it fit for a king. You are the king that reigns in your home. What kind of home are you, as a king, ruling over?

There are some exceptions to the rule of every man having his own home to rule over. Because of certain circumstances that happen in life, some men may be living with their parents or with someone else. Some young men are still in school and living in their parents' home. Some men may have moved back to their parents' home to care for a sick loved one. Others may have had setbacks in life and may have had to move in with someone. In most of these cases, living in someone else's home should be a temporary situation in which he is working to change.

C. A man, if he is married with children, is to have dominion and authority over his wife and family.

If he is married but has no children, he is to be the head of his wife. A man is to have dominion and authority over himself, over his home, and over those who live within his home. Having dominion over those in his home does not mean he dominates them as a dictator; it means he rules over them as Christ rules over the church. If a man does not exercise dominion and authority in the same manner as Christ does, he is not exercising it as God expects him to. As a king in your home, what kind of a king and ruler are you? Are you a just, gentle, and loving king like Jesus Christ? Are you the type of king your wife and children are glad to be subject to? To have dominion and authority is great only when it is used in a good, godly, and Christ-like way.

While a man has the God-given right to exercise dominion and authority in certain areas, he must realize that at times he must come under the dominion and authority of others. He is under the dominion and authority of the state and country in which he lives. He is under the dominion and authority of the police force of the state and country in which he lives. He may be under the authority of an employer and supervisor. He should be under the authority of a pastor and church leaders. One of the greatest responsibilities that come with exercising dominion and authority is responding properly to those who may have dominion and authority over you.

[17] Obey them that have the rule over you, and submit yourselves: for they watch for your souls, as they that must give account, that they may do it with joy, and not with grief: for that is unprofitable for you. (Hebrews.13:17)

4. A man is to be a person that works (Genesis. 3:19, 2 Thessalonians. 3:10, Ephesians. 4:28).

*A. A man is to work for money
so he can provide for his own.*

A man, who will be the type of man God wants him to be, must be a man who provides for his own.

[8.] But if any provide not for his own, and specially for those of his own house, he hath denied the faith, and is worse than an infidel. (1st Timothy.5:8)

The way God ordained for him to provide for his own is for him to work. While *work* is a four-letter word, it is not a bad word. God worked during the Creation, Jesus worked to redeem men (John 17:4), and God gave Adam work to do in the Garden of Eden. God gave Adam the work of (1) keeping the garden, (2) having dominion over the animals, (3) having dominion over all the earthly creations, and (4) naming all of the animals. Work is something God did, and it is something God has ordained for men to do.

It is not a sin for a woman to work and even make more money than her husband, but it is a sin for a man not to work at all (if he is able to work). God makes special provisions for a man who is unable to work because of a mental or physical illness. Sickness is an acceptable reason in the sight of

God for a man to refrain from working; however, that sickness must be to the point where the man just can't perform any type of work. If he is sick but can safely perform some kind of work (and can get a job), he is to do it.

There are some men who stays home with the children while the wife goes out to work. These men are called "*Mr. Mom*". This is not an acceptable practice in the eyes of God. God tells the man to be the provider (1st Timothy.5:8) and the woman to be the nurturer of the children (1st Timothy.5:10). If a man wants to stay at home with the children while the wife goes out to work, that man needs to find a business that he can work from his home. While the Bible does not say he has to make more money than his wife, it does say that he has to provide something for his own. The man is to work from home, or go to work after his wife gets home, but he is to work if he is going to be the type of man God desires him to be.

Work gives a man a sense of purpose, worth and accomplishment. A sense of being worth something and being able to accomplish something are traits God puts into a man to prompt him to always be working. It is not the work itself that makes a man worth something (all men are of great worth to God whether they work or not); work just gives him a sense of being needed and valued for what he can do. A great and tragic mistake that many employers and wives often make is the mistake of making a man feel worthless and unneeded.

B. A man is to always do good works that shows he is a child of God.

While a man is to do some kind of physical work that will bring finances into the home, there are other kinds of works that God wants a man to perform. A man is to always do good works that show he is a child of God. He may not receive finances for it, but God will reward him. The works of righteousness a saint should be performing include helping others in need, doing acts of kindness to people on a regular basis, speaking only clean and wholesome things, and always seeking to do what is right while avoiding doing what is wrong in the eyes of God. All of these things should be done in such ways that they ultimately give glory to God.

C. A man is to always be doing work for the kingdom of Christ.

He is to work for God in the church (choir member, deacon, teacher, usher, janitor, etc.), and he is to work for God outside the church (witnessing, visiting the sick, helping the needy, feeding the hungry to the glory of God, passing out tracts, etc.). He is to work for God in his home (praying, teaching his wife and children God's Word, home Bible studies with friends, etc.). Working for money and for the kingdom of God, is the kind of work a man must do if he is to be the kind of man God desires him to be.

D. A man is to work at home.

A man is to work for money, a man is to work for God, and a man is to work at home. He should be constantly working around the home to make his home the best it can be. He is to help keep it clean, neat, and as beautiful as possible. He is to continually work on his marriage to make it the best it can be. Marriages are like houses—if you do not do regular maintenance on them, over time, they will fall apart. Many marriages are falling apart because many husbands have neglected doing the regular maintenance work needed to keep a marriage together.

E. A man is to also work on raising his children in the nurture and admonition of the Lord.

4 And, ye fathers, provoke not your children to wrath: but bring them up in the nurture and admonition of the Lord. (Ephesians. 6:4)

He should be the one seeking their souls' salvation and instructing them in the Word of God. He is to teach them how to pray, and he should constantly pray for them and with them. The life of a man is to be a busy life because it is to be a life filled with work.

F. A man is to work on himself.

A man is to work for money, a man is to work for God, a man is to work for his family, and a man is to work on himself. One of the worst things a man can do to himself is to "let himself go" physically, mentally, spiritually, and emotionally. If you are going to be the type of man God wants you to be, you must always be working on yourself. You should seek to look your best, you should seek to grow spiritually, and you should seek to show the proper emotions of love to your wife and family that God tells you to show. Don't expect others to cause you to do those things; it is you who must work on yourself so you can become the man God wants you to be.

Father; becoming saved, living for You, and growing more and more into what You desire me to be, has been the greatest thing I have ever done. I once hated who I was; but now I love who You have made me into. Being who You say I am, is the best I am, that I can be. In Jesus' name I pray; amen.

Jesus my LORD; the more I become who the Father wants me to become, the more I become like You. I truly want to be like You.

Jesus is LORD

CHAPTER 19

What Is a Man, and What Is a Man Supposed to Do? (Part 2)

5. A man is to be one who knows how to humble himself under the authority of others (1st Corinthians. 11:3, Philippians. 2:5-8, Hebrews. 2:6-7).

6. A man is to be one who is meek (Matthew. 5:5, Matthew. 11:29, Numbers. 12:3).
   A. A meek person is a person who seeks to put God (and the ways of God) first in everything.
   B. A meek person is a person who seeks to obey the call of God upon his life.
   C. A meek person is a person who is not proud in spirit.
   D. A meek person is one who serves God by serving others.
   E. A meek person is one who desires for others to be as great as he is or greater than he is.

7. A man is to be the spiritual head and high priest of his home (1st Peter. 2:9).
   A. As the spiritual head and high priest of his family he is to be a man of prayer and the one who leads the way in being a Christian example for his family.
   B. As the spiritual leader and high priest of his home, he is to lead the way in teaching his family the Word of God.

C. As the spiritual head and high priest of his home, he leads the way in spiritual service to God.

8. A man is to be the protector and defender of his family and home (Ephesians. 6:10-18).

9. A man is to be a decision maker (James 5:12).

10. A man is to be a romantic lover who loves and romances his wife only (Song of Solomon).

5. A man is to be one who knows how to humble himself under the authority of others (1st Corinthians.11:3, Philippians. 2:5-8, Hebrews. 2:6-7).

In order for a man to properly understand having authority, he must understand being under authority (Matthew.8:1-10). A man is under the authority of Christ, he is under the authority of his pastor, he is under the authority of his boss, and he is under the authority of the nation and state in which he lives. It is not wrong, it is not a sin, and it is not a shame to be under the authority of others. Being under the authority of others is only a natural part of God's order of things.

A good leader must first become a good follower, a good ruler must first be a good subject, and a good teacher must first be a good student. How you act under the authority of others will show what type of person you will be when you are in authority. A person who is unfaithful and unjust with that which belongs to another; will be unfaithful and unjust with that which belongs to himself. If you are going to be the type of man God wants you to be, you must learn to be a man who submits under the authority of others.

6. A man is to be one who is meek (Matthew. 5:5, Matthew. 11:29, Numbers. 12:3).

While society says a man is to be brave, macho, and is to show no emotions, God says a man is to be meek, humble, and harmless. To be meek does not mean to be weak and cowardly. To be meek means "although you are strong, mighty, and powerful," you are yet more concerned about the needs, rights, and well-being of others than you are about yourself. It means to be kind, compassionate, gentle, and understanding while doing what is just, right, and fair in your dealings with people. While you care for the needs of others, you refuse to let people take advantage of you and constantly misuse you. You guard against being misused because while you are as harmless as a dove, you are as wise as a serpent. If you are going to be the type of man God says a man should be, you must develop a personality of meekness.

In order to develop a personality of meekness, one must learn what the characteristics of meekness are, and then he must learn how to implement those characteristics into his personality. Although Moses was a powerful and strong leader, he was called the meekest man on earth

³ Now the man Moses was very meek, above all the men which were upon the face of the earth. (Numbers. 12:3).

We can learn what meekness is and how to develop meekness in our lives by studying the lifestyle and leadership ability of Moses.

A. A meek person is a person who seeks to put God (and the ways of God) first in everything.

The major desire in the heart of Moses was to obey God, and to see the purposes of God accomplished. Moses loved his God so much that he *²⁴ "refused to be called the son of Pharaoh's daughter, ²⁵ choosing rather to suffer affliction with the people of God, than to enjoy the pleasures of sin for a season; ²⁶ Esteeming the reproach of Christ greater riches than the treasures in Egypt"* (Hebrews.11:24-26).

Moses had the highest regards possible for his God and the ways of his God. Moses sinned at times, and did things the wrong way, but the major desires of his heart and life were to see the will of God accomplished. If you are going to develop a personality of meekness, you must develop a personality of wanting to put God first in everything. You may sin at times and do wrong things, but the overall desire of your heart must be to put God first in everything.

B. A meek person is a person who seeks to obey the call of God upon his life.

Although Moses was somewhat afraid to fulfill the call of God to go and deliver the children of Israel out of Egyptian bondage, he rose above his fears and became obedient to his God. When you know God is laying something on your heart to do, if you are going to develop a personality of meekness, you must obey what God is telling you to do. The meek will humble themselves and obey God. Only a prideful, stubborn, and hard-hearted person rebels against God and the call of God on his life.

C. A meek person is a person who is not proud in spirit.

A person who possesses an attitude of meekness is one who does not possess an attitude of pride and arrogance. He is one who does not think he is better than others. When God called Moses to deliver the children of Israel out of Egyptian bondage, Moses thought very lowly of himself and asked, *"Who am I, that I should go unto Pharaoh and that I should bring forth the children of Israel out of Egypt?" (Exodus.3:11).* Moses was not a man who felt that he was competent enough to accomplish great things. He knew of his shortcomings and that if he was to do anything great, it would be because God was working in him.

Are you filled with self-confidence? Do you feel you can accomplish all things because of who you are and what you possess? If this is the type of attitude you possess, you are proud, you are arrogant, and you lack the great quality of meekness. A meek person is one who knows he can only accomplish things by the power of God, and he has great trust in, and great dependency on God.

D. A meek person is one who serves God by serving others.

The legacy left by the life of Moses was a legacy of service to his God and a legacy of service to God's people. Moses did nothing for self-glory or self-gain. All that he did was aimed toward fulfilling the service God called him to do. The only way to fulfill that service was to give his life to serving other people. He served people by delivering them out of Egypt. He served people by providing for their needs (through the power of God) while they were in the wilderness. He served them by guiding them, teaching them, praying for them, and interceding for them. The meekness that was the predominate force of Moses' character showed forth by his many acts of service to his God and to other people.

What service are you rendering to others? How can you truly say you are serving God when you are not serving others? If you want to develop a personality of meekness, you must develop an attitude of service to others. When you see people in need and you have the power and opportunity to help them, if you are a meek person, you will do what you can to help.

E. A meek person is one who desires others to be as great as he is, or greater than he is.

God had placed His unique Holy Spirit in Moses so that Moses could lead the children of Israel. There came a time when God was going to pour that same Spirit on seventy of the elders of Israel. Moses was so meek and humble that he wished that God would pour His Spirit upon all of the people of Israel (Numbers. 11:29). Moses wanted everyone to be as great as he was.

7. A man is to be the spiritual head and high priest of his home (1st Peter.2:9).

If a man is going to be the kind of man God wants him to be, he must become the spiritual head and high priest of his home. To be the spiritual head and high priest of his home means that he is the one who takes responsibility for the spiritual well-being of his family. He takes the leadership role in spiritual things, and is the most active in spiritual affairs. For a man who is trying to be the kind of man God wants him to be, being the spiritual head and high priest of his family is not a passive thing for him; it is the major goal of his life.

A. As the spiritual head and high priest of his family he is to be a man of prayer and the one who leads the way in being a Christian example for his family.

As a Christian example, he seeks to learn how a saint is supposed to live, and then he tries with all of his heart to live that way in the eyes of his family. He lives his life in such a way that his family can tell he has a deep and personal relationship with the Lord Jesus Christ. They can tell that Jesus is actively involved in his life and that his life is centered on God. Before any spiritual high priest can share his religion with others, it must first be seen that it is lived out in his life. Are you the spiritual high priest of your home? Are you leading the way in the spiritual affairs of your family?

As the spiritual leader and high priest of his home, he is to lead the way in family prayer and devotions. His family should be able to tell that he is a man of prayer, because they often see him praying. He is the one responsible for teaching his family how to pray, and he is the one responsible for calling the family together for times of family prayer. It is impossible to be the spiritual high priest in your home if you are not a man of prayer.

B. As the spiritual leader and high priest of his home, he is to lead the way in teaching his family the Word of God.

He first learns it himself, and then gathers the family together to teach them the things he has learned. He teaches them how to apply it in their lives, and to always obey it. He tells them the rewards of obeying God's Word and the tragedies that follow those who disobey. He reassures them that the Holy Bible comes from God, and that it is the foundation they need to build their lives on. As the spiritual leader and high priest of his home, a godly kind of man never omits nor neglects the Word of God.

C. As the spiritual head and high priest of his home, he leads the way in spiritual service to God.

He makes sure his family is in church every Sunday. He takes them to Sunday school and Bible study. He lets his family know that God requires spiritual service; and part of that service includes gathering weekly with other saints in praise, worship, and study of the Word of God. He shows his family that giving to God is also a part of one's spiritual service. He gives of his finances and his time. He gives of his possession, talents, and abilities. He gives what he can, when he can, and he does it with a heart of love for his God and for others. A spiritual high priest knows there are spiritual services to perform, and he leads the way in performing them.

8. A man is to be the protector and defender of his family and home (Ephesians. 6:10-18).

Many physical and spiritual enemies will come to attack the home and family of every man. These enemies are strong, and they are wicked. Their major goals for coming are to steal, kill, and destroy. As a man over his home, you are to be the one responsible for protecting your family against all physical and spiritual enemies. Your wife and family should feel secure in knowing that you are there to protect them. You may not be able to destroy all of the enemies, but your family should know that you would give your life trying. They should know you would do all that is within your power to protect them and to keep them from harm and danger.

As a protector of the home, you should seek to keep your home safe from outside intruders. You cannot always stop burglars and robbers, but your family should know that you have made your home as secure as possible. They should know that while you are there, you would fight anyone who would try to invade your home.

Not only are you to protect them from burglars and robbers, you are to protect them from bill collectors, harassing individuals, unscrupulous salespersons, and anyone who may come to the home with a harsh and negative attitude and demeanor. Such people as these, after talking to you, will know that you will never tolerate anyone upsetting or disturbing your wife emotionally, and that they must talk to you and not your wife about any business they may have. You stand as watchman over your home, and you keep at bay all who may seek to harm your family or to bring them discomfort.

You are to also protect your family from the spiritual enemies that come and try to tempt them into doing things against the Word and will of God. The devil and his demons will come and try to tempt you and your family members into doing wrong things. You are never to yield to the temptations of the devil. Never be the one the devil is using to do wrong, but always strive to be the one God is using to do what is right. You are responsible for telling your family when they are doing wrong, and you are not to tolerate any sinful behavior in your home. A protector is not just one who protects from physical enemies only, but he is also one who protects from spiritual enemies as well.

9. A man is to be a decision maker. (James.1:5-8)

A man should be one who knows how to make decisions, and he should be one who is willing to deal with the consequences of the decisions he makes. One of the major qualities that a leader must possess is the ability to make decisions. He must learn how to make the wisest decisions possible, and how to make decisions that do not violate the written Word of God. He should get input from his wife before making any major decisions, and they should both be in agreement over the decisions he makes. He is not to be a double-minded person, who wavers back and forth over an issue. He needs to be decisive and to be able to make wise decisions about things.

[12] But above all things, my brethren, swear not, neither by heaven, neither by the earth, neither by any other oath: **_but let your yea be yea; and your nay, nay; lest ye fall into condemnation._** *(James.5:12)*

There may come times when a man will make a decision that may not turn out very well for him and his family. All men will make mistakes. When confronted with an un-profitable decision you have made, you must be willing to deal with the consequences that may occur. Don't regret making the decision; just seek God on how to turn a bad decision into a blessed one. Learn from them, overcome them, and profit from them. It is not the bad decisions with their consequences that matters the most, but it is your reaction to bad decisions and how you overcome them, that matters the most.

10. A man is to be a romantic lover who loves and romances his wife only (Song of Solomon.).

I believe that the Bible book of the Song of Solomon was included in the Bible for two major reasons: (1) to show the love relationship Christ has with His bride the church, and (2) to let men know God wants them to be romantic lovers of their own wives. Christian men are to be as much like Christ as they can. Because Jesus Christ romantically loves His church, Christian men should romantically love their wives. If you are going to be the kind of man God wants you to be, you must (if you are married) be a man of romance.

Romance in marriage includes five major things:

1. Telling her of your love for her.
2. Doing things to show your love for her.
3. Telling her how beautiful she is in your eyes.
4. Doing these things constantly.
5. Constantly increasing in doing these things.

Romance in marriage starts at the beginning of the marriage, and should continue until the day you or she dies. It is something that should never decrease, nor totally vanish away.

Romance in marriage should be fun, exciting, and refreshing. It should be an adventure into ecstasy that begins with verbal compliments, and then moves up to romantic gestures, and ends in physical and emotional fulfillment and enjoyment. It is a task that must be worked at, worked on, and constantly updated. Romance in marriage can never be taken for granted nor should it ever be neglected. Romance in marriage is a lifetime duty that every husband should perform and should perform constantly if he is going to be the kind of man God wants him to be.

Father; no husband or man will ever know their true purpose in life until they become what You instruct them to become, and do all You command them to do. True fulfillment in life is being saved, loving You, trusting You, worshiping You, living Your way, and doing as You command. Thank You for empowering me and all yielded husbands and men, to have a fulfilling life. In Jesus' name I pray; amen.

Jesus my LORD; it is only because of You that my life is enriched, fulfilling, and worth living. Thank You for giving me the best life I could possibly live.

Jesus is LORD

CHAPTER 20

Spiritual Checklists for Husbands and Men

Performance evaluation reviews are a normal part of life. From early in one's life to the latter years of one's existence, he is constantly confronted with performance evaluation reviews. Starting in elementary school and continuing through graduate school, students constantly have to deal with performance evaluation reviews. These reviews come in the form of tests. At work, there are performance evaluation reviews that come in the form of job performance evaluations that employers give regularly. Regardless of who you are or what level of accomplishments you may have achieved, you will sooner or later be confronted with some kind of performance evaluation review.

Performance reviews are an excellent way for a person to be evaluated on how well they are performing at a certain task. It is also an excellent way of determining how well they will perform at a future task they may be confronted with. One of the greatest and most important tasks that a man will be confronted with in this life is the task of being a husband and a father. How good are you at being a husband? What guidelines will you use to determine how good or bad a husband you are? Are you willing to take a husband performance evaluation based on the Word of God? Are you willing to evaluate your marriage to see how strong or how weak a marriage you have?

We have developed a series of questions based on the Word of God, and based upon the things taught in this book. We believe these questions will help you to gauge your performance as a husband, and will also help you to determine how strong your marriage is. Oftentimes, a husband will think he is doing great as a husband, but he will never really know how good or how bad a husband he is until he stops to look at himself, and measure himself according to the Word of God.

We are often evaluated on things that we consider important in life; therefore, I feel that husbands should be evaluated on one of the most important things in life. That most important thing is our performance as husbands and fathers. These questions are divided into different categories that are taken from different sections of this book. They deal with you and your relationship with God, you and your relationship with your wife, you and your relationship with your children, and you and your relationship with yourself.

This evaluation section will show you areas in which you may need to improve if you are going to improve on strengthening your marriage. The stronger you are in certain areas, the stronger your marriage will be. This evaluation of you is not to be done once and then forgotten about. You are to regularly take this evaluation and constantly review your performance as a husband and as a father. We as husbands oftentimes allow things to slip, but this constant evaluation will help you to guard against slipping back into habits of neglecting your God-given duties as a man, a husband, and a father.

Jesus is LORD

Aelton Simmons

SPIRITUAL CHECKLIST

	Yes	No
1. Are you a Christian husband?		
2. Can your family tell by your lifestyle that you are a dedicated Christian?		
3. Do you pray at least three times a day?		
4. Do you daily lead your family in prayer?		
5. Do you read and meditate on the Word of God daily?		
6. Do you teach the Word of God to your family?		
7. Do you attend church every week (or almost every week) with your family?		
8. Do you perform a Christian service (deacon, Bible teacher, usher, choir member, soul winner, etc.)?		
9. Do you and your wife often discuss the Word of God together?		
10. Do you and your wife work together in some kind of Christian service?		
11. Do you ever go on a fast?		
12. Do you still live a dedicated Christian life even when no one can see what you are doing?		
13. When you commit a sin, do you quickly repent of the sin, and then go forward seeking to live the best Christian lifestyle you can?		

God's Divine Instructions To Husbands and Men

COMMUNICATION CHECKLIST

	Yes	No
1. Have you consistently tried to develop and maintain a time for you and your wife to communicate daily?		
2. Are there times when you just listen to your wife without trying to give answers and advice?		
3. Does your wife feel comfortable with sharing her heart with you?		
4. Is there a special time for communication between you and the children?		
5. Do your kids feel comfortable communicating with you?		
6. Are you able to hold your temper when you are angry, and not say things you will later regret saying?		
7. When angry, do you refrain from cursing and from name-calling?		
8. When angry, do you keep from raising your voice?		
9. When angry, do you try to wait until you calm down before engaging in any meaningful conversation?		
10. Do you get angry very often?		
11. Is your speech always "with grace, seasoned with salt (Colossians. 4:6)"?		

12. Do you daily speak words of romance, love, and compliments to your wife—words like "I love you," "You look good today," "You are a great wife," "You are a great mother," "I am so happy I am married to you," etc.?		
13. Do you give nonverbal acts of communication of love and appreciation to your wife?		
14. Do you ever say to your wife words like "I was wrong," "I'm sorry," "Please forgive me," or "Honey, I should have listened to you, you were right"?		
15. Have you developed the art of knowing when it is the best time to communicate and when it's not a good time to communicate?		
16. Do you constantly encourage and edify your wife concerning the things she endeavors to do?		

God's Divine Instructions To Husbands and Men

ACTS OF LOVE AND APPRECIATION CHECKLIST

	Yes	No
1. Do you remember special occasions (anniversaries, birthdays, and holidays) and do special things for your wife on those days?		
2. Do you do unexpected special things for your wife "just because"?		
3. Do you set aside a certain day once a week or twice a week to do special things with your wife (going out to dinner, taking her shopping, walking together, watching movies, etc.)?		
4. Do you help your wife with housework and with the children?		
5. Do you give your wife roses, candies, and romantic cards regularly?		
6. Do you seek to find what your wife's desires are and then seek to fulfill them?		
7. Do you include your wife in your world (your hobbies and friends) and also seek to find hobbies that you and she can enjoy together?		
8. Do you seek to make your wife feel like she is a special woman of notable excellence?		
9. Do you give your wife hugs and kisses when romance and sex is not the aim?		
10. Do you seek to love your wife like Christ loves the church and to treat her like Christ treats His bride, the church?		

Aelton Simmons

HUSBAND'S DUTY CHECKLIST FROM 1st Corinthians 7

	Yes	No
1. (vs. 2) Do you have your own wife and her only (are you being faithful to your wife)?		
2. (vs. 3) Do you seek to give to your wife due benevolence (all of the services that God says is due a wife)?		
3. (vs. 4) Have you yielded full control of your body to your wife (can she tell you things to do and things not to do with your body, and you obey her)?		
4. (vs. 5) Do you seek to fulfill your wife's sexual needs regularly?		
5. (vs. 5) Do you seek to do the best you can for your wife sexually?		
6. (vs. 5) Are you a man of fasting and prayer?		
7. (vs. 11) Have you made a commitment to stay married to your wife for a lifetime (never leave her nor force her to leave you for non-biblical reasons)?		
8. (vs. 11) If your wife leaves (or has already left) you, will you work hard at trying to get her to come back?		
9. (vs. 14) Do you try to live a sanctified and holy life for your wife and children?		
10. (vs. 16) Are you doing all you can to seek to get your wife and children saved?		
11. (vs. 33) Do you do all you can to seek to please your wife?		

God's Divine Instructions To Husbands and Men

HUSBAND'S DUTY CHECKLIST FROM EPHESIANS 5

	Yes	No
1. (vs. 25) Do you seek to love your wife like Christ loves His bride, the church?		
2. (vs. 25) Do you seek to treat your wife like Christ treats His bride, the church?		
3. (vs. 25) Do you seek to lead your wife (be the head of her) like Christ leads (is the head of) His bride, the church?		
4. (vs. 25) Have you given yourself for your wife (dedicated your life to her) and make the greatest sacrifices you can for her?		
5. (vs. 27) Are you helping your wife to become the best person she can become?		
6. (vs. 28) Do you love your wife as you love your own body?		
7. (vs. 29) Do you nourish and cherish your wife?		
8. (vs. 31) Do you consider you and your wife as one (one person, one body)?		

Aelton Simmons

HUSBAND'S DUTY CHECKLIST FROM COLOSSIANS 3:19 AND 1st PETER 3:7

From Colossians 3:19	Yes	No
1. (vs. 19) Do you love your wife (and does it show by what you do and by what you say)?		
2. (vs. 19) Do you do all you can to keep from being bitter against your wife (even when she does things to make you bitter, and when you feel you have a right to be bitter)?		
3. From 1st Peter 3:7		
4. (vs. 7) Do you seek to dwell with your wife according to the knowledge given you in the Word of God?		
5. (vs. 7) Do you seek to dwell with your wife according to the knowledge of the things you've learned about her (according to her likes, her dislikes, her wants, her desires, and her expectations for you as her husband)?		
6. (vs. 7) Do you give your wife the greatest honor that you can?		
7. (vs. 7) Do you allow your wife to be the weaker vessel (express her emotions)?		
8. (vs. 7) Do you live your life knowing that the greatest blessings God is giving you (other than salvation) He is giving you because you are married to her?		

God's Divine Instructions To Husbands and Men

THINGS TO AVOID CHECKLIST

	Yes	No
1. Do you totally refrain from slapping, hitting, abusing, or doing anything to your wife that brings mental or physical pain?		
2. Do you refrain from cheating on your wife?		
3. Do you refrain from lying to your wife?		
4. Do you refrain from embarrassing your wife before others?		
5. Do you refrain from saying bad things about your wife?		
6. Do you refrain from discussing with others the things that happen in your bedroom?		
7. Do you refrain from putting anyone or anything before your wife but God?		
8. Do you refrain from taking the romance out of your marriage? Do you still date your wife?		
9. Do you do all you can to try to keep your love for your wife from dying?		

Aelton Simmons

THE HUSBAND'S LOVEMAKING CHECKLIST

	Yes	No
1. Are you sensitive to the changes in your wife's sexual needs?		
2. Are you doing all you can to keep your wife's emotional feelings for you strong so her physical fulfillment by you can be the best it can be for her?		
3. Do you work to bring your wife mental and emotional peace and security before you see to bring her physical fulfillment?		
4. Do you work throughout the day to get your wife ready for romance at the end of the day?		
5. Are you more concerned about pleasing your wife than being pleased by her?		
6. Do you work hard to keep romance in your marriage?		
7. Are you understanding of your wife when you really desire lovemaking and she says, "Not tonight"?		
8. Do you place more emphasis on loving your wife than on making love to her?		
9. Do you pray, asking God's blessing to be on you and your wife when it's time for you and her to make love together?		
10. Do you guard against sexual routines?		
11. Do you engage in mental, emotional, and physical foreplay before making love to your wife?		

12. Do you ask your wife if she is really being satisfied and fulfilled when you and she are making love?		
13. Do you ask your wife what she would like to do when it comes to making love?		
14. Do you seek to find out what your wife likes and then major on doing those things (as long as it is not anything that violates your conscience)?		
15. Do you abstain from asking your wife to do anything that violates her conscience?		

Father; thank You for blessing me, and anointing me, to write this book. Please use it for Your glory. In Jesus' name I pray; amen.

Jesus my LORD; I trust this book into Your hands. Your will be done concerning it. I love You my Lord and Savior. Thank You so much for using me in this project.

Jesus is LORD

www.ingramcontent.com/pod-product-compliance
Lightning Source LLC
Chambersburg PA
CBHW020523080526
44583CB00013B/711